"WHAT IS NOT"
and
"WHAT IS"

CULTIVATING PEACE OF MIND AND INNER FREEDOM;

AN EXPLORATION IN THE PRACTICE OF DISCRIMINATING WISDOM

by

David D. V. Fisher, PhD.

 FriesenPress

Suite 300 - 990 Fort St
Victoria, BC, V8V 3K2
Canada

www.friesenpress.com

ISBN
978-1-03-910259-0 (Hardcover)
978-1-03-910258-3 (Paperback)
978-1-03-910260-6 (eBook)

1. Psychology, Cognitive Psychology

Distributed to the trade by The Ingram Book Company

ACKNOWLEDGMENTS & DEDICATION

I want to thank the members of our meditation group, The Nanaimo Dharma Practice Group, for contributing year-long through their reading of the draft text, then applying the suggested practices and providing feedback. I received their comments with gratitude and made ample use of them. I thank you all.

Gisele Benoit, Lisa Brosseau, Susan Fisher, David Hay and Heather Marshall, my principal editor, everyone of you contributed so much to the preparation of this book. I deeply appreciate all of your support and assistance. I thank you.

May this work be of benefit to all who contributed to its writing, as well as to all who read this book. May you discover a way of thinking that assists you to cultivate emotional and personal well-being – lifelong. May your well-being bring benefit to everyone touched by your presence.

David Fisher,
2021-02-28

PREVIOUS PUBLICATIONS BY DAVID FISHER

An Introduction to Constructivism for Social Workers. Praeger, 1991.

The Silken Thread. Self-published through Trafford, 2007.

SECRETS – Communication, Language, and Intimacy. Self-published through First Choice Books, 2011.

PREFACE

Knowledge and Wisdom

All that we know we learned in the past. Too often, we use that Knowledge to define the present. When we act according to the certainties of our own defining, we recreate the past in the present and too often foredoom the future.

Alternatively, we may cultivate Wisdom by setting aside our definitions, staying present to our experience and use knowledge skillfully to bring forth a beneficial future. In this way, we make our knowledge our servant rather than allowing it to continue as our master.

dvf
2007-12-14

CONTENTS

INTRODUCTION

Let me tell you that you are deluded. You are deluded by living in 'What Is Not." How did you take the statement, "You're deluded." Did you notice what you thought? If you reacted in any way, like, "What's this 'What Is Not' nonsense!" "Who does he think he is?" "Nuts! I am not deluded," or even, "Well, I probably am deluded, at least sometimes," no matter what your reaction, it came from "What Is Not."

On the other hand if you noticed, "Oh. I am reacting," or sensed curiosity and just moved on and continued reading, you were with "What Is." You responded to your immediate experience and flowed with it. Throughout this book I refer to "immediate experience" intending to emphasize what is going on for you right now. I am not referring to your historical or overall experience.

A theme of this book is to invite you to attend to your immediate experience, starting by distinguishing **reactivity** from *responding*. I begin with this distinction because you, as reader, can easily recognize reactivity and responsiveness in yourself, and self-observation is crucial to making use of the ideas presented. Learning to shift from reacting to responding makes the difference between living with mental and emotional distress and cultivating peace of mind and a sense of inner freedom.

Our reactivity derives from mental habits and emotions that separate us from one another and our environment. Feelings of separateness are key to emotional distress. Responsiveness expresses our connectedness in the moment and cultivating a sense of connection is crucial to our well-being. Reactivity and responding are explored in Chapter One. Here, I want to emphasize why reactivity is such an important marker.

All our reactivity results from encountering life events, including our own thinking, through the lens of defining, that is "What Is Not." **Having defined any event, we then act in relation to our definitions, not our immediate experience.** In this way we live according to "What Is Not." Reactivity is essential to protect us physically, as in avoiding tigers. But socially we create unwarranted distress within ourselves and quite frequently affect other people, for instance, by dwelling on worries.

Most of our distress is born of habitual ways of thinking, no matter how much we believe that our distress is caused by external events and life circumstances. An alternative resides in a shift in perspective. In making this shift we learn to alleviate distress and to cultivate peace of mind and a sense of inner freedom. That is what this book is about.

Ordinarily, we dwell in "What Is Not," living at the dictate of our beliefs. This is normal for us, and we rarely even notice how our beliefs run our lives. When we shift our perspective, we use the "What Is" of our immediate experience as our basis for action. We make this shift by practicing *Discriminating Wisdom*. We will explore this concept and associated practices throughout this book. The intent of this book is to assist you in making this shift. I have used a metaphor describing contrasting forest paths to illustrate the shift.

FOREST PATHS

Think of us living in a great forest. In this forest, we tramp around a well-worn path. We have been tramping around it for many years. Surely there are seasonal differences, and growth here, and death and disease there. Even so we trip over the same roots time after time. We get hooked by the same briars, mired in the same muddy patches, and collide with the same boulders over and over again. Following this path, we distress ourselves. Yet habitually we blame the roots, briars, the rain, and the rocks for our distress. We may question the path we follow, but we follow it just the same. This represents the "What Is Not" of our lives.

However, there is an alternative path available to us in every moment. ***This is a path we lay by walking it.*** We lay this path by engaging directly with the "What Is" of our immediate experience. We attend to present-time experiences skillfully by practicing Discriminating Wisdom.

As we lay our path walking, the roots we encounter are core beliefs that became well established in our earliest years. Although they provide stability, they also present obstacles. We can learn to stop tripping over them. The briars bear the thorns of our ego-identities. We still encounter briars, but, at the same time, we are learning not to get hooked on the thorns of ego. Perhaps we will encounter muddy patches such as depression, anxiety, or confusion. We learn to fill them in and not get bogged down anymore.

Then there are the boulders. We come smack up against the rock-hardness of our beliefs, the massive nature of our egos and the weight and burden of our habitual ways of thinking. We experience our boulders as resistance to making the shifts we need to make if we are to alleviate distress. In laying our own path, we learn to appreciate the boulders, and in appreciating them – amazingly and over time – they are reduced to pebbles. All these things we learn by practicing *Discriminating Wisdom.*

DISCRIMINATING WISDOM

Discriminating Wisdom combines knowledge, skills and understanding, enabling us to tell the difference between "What Is Not" and *"What Is,"* and how to use these contrasting perspectives to cultivate peace of mind and inner freedom.

There is nothing magical in this process, and there is no quick fix. This book can only offer signposts and guidelines. It is your power and your energy that is needed to engage in the process of retraining your brain if you are to cultivate both peace of mind and a sense of inner freedom, no matter what else is going on in your life.

It is your power and your energy that is needed to engage in the process of retraining your brain if you are to cultivate both peace of mind and a sense of inner freedom.

The practice of *Discriminating Wisdom* entails *making a lifelong commitment to your own well-being.* I am not suggesting that you make a commitment now, like a promise to yourself. Commitment is cultivated through practice: it becomes a way of being – nothing more, nothing less.

"Discriminating Wisdom" is a Buddhist concept (Pali: "Pañña, or in Sanskrit: prajña).[1] In Buddhist terms, this is a fundamental teaching towards enlightenment. What I am offering is a broad interpretation using modern perspectives on language, communication, brain science, psychology, and evolution. With practice, you will recognize when you are dwelling in "What Is Not." You will know when you are present to "What Is" and cultivate the wisdom to walk on this earth with peace of mind and a sense of inner freedom.

Practicing *Discriminating Wisdom* is not to dismiss "What Is Not." To the contrary, acting within "What Is Not" not only supports our survival, but it is essential to many of our social and economic activities. "What Is Not" provides a rich variety to our lives as well as a measure of security. Yet so long as we invest our identities, our sense of mattering as persons, in "What Is Not," we continue to experience emotional distress.

---

1 Pañña (Pali) or prajña (Sanskrit) "wisdom" is insight into the true nature of reality, namely primarily anicca (impermanence), dukkha (dissatisfaction or suffering), anatta (non-self) and sunyata (emptiness). Wikipedia: https://en.wikipedia.org/wiki/Praj%C3%B1%C4%81_%28Buddhism%29

CULTIVATING BENEFIT

I indicated earlier that I offer signposts, guidelines, and practices as well as the reasoning underlying them. Even so, please do not take these ideas as being intended as "The Truth" or "The Answer." Rather take them in the light of The Buddha's instruction to the Kalama people (*Kalamasutta*). The gist of this *sutta*[2] is: Do not take any teaching on blind faith no matter who the authority is. Rather, test it out experientially. Does following the instruction lead to benefit or to harm to you as well as other people whose lives you touch? If you find it beneficial, adopt it as an ongoing practice. If it leads to harm (distress), dump it!

On the other hand, if you hope for miracles, you may drop a practice prematurely. How much we practice, and what we practice makes the difference. This contrasts with the gratification we have learned to expect from our cellphones, related technologies, and the vast range of consumer goods available to us. If we are to ameliorate emotional distress and dissatisfaction, we need to recognize that we are not machines. Rather we are living organisms with a great capacity for learning. We learn our patterns of behavior and thought as powerful habits. Some of these habits generate distress. However, we can draw on the same capacity for learning to cultivate new habits of thinking and acting. We must release many of our urges for short-term gratification to achieve beneficial outcomes in the longer-term.

The Buddha used wording that we translate as "benefit" and "beneficial." The intention underlying all the practices recommended in this book is to cultivate benefit. What counts as "beneficial" is longer-term ways of being for the months and years ahead. "Ways of being" refers to processes, not states. Examples of such processes include sustaining physical health and emotional well-being, practicing being at peace within one's self and maintaining mutually rewarding relationships with a number of other people.

We can also benefit by reducing stress and managing stressors successfully. We forgive ourselves and other people, where forgiveness is essentially putting down any burdens we carry from the past. Likewise, we benefit by identifying and releasing beliefs that bind us into distress.

The principle "cultivate benefit" represents the direction in which to make effort. I do not intend this book to be read with any sense of a guaranteed outcome. Cultivation is an ongoing process. As with gardening, the plants give us feedback. We cultivate our garden accordingly. Likewise, as part of a process of observation and learning, we also cultivate *Discriminating Wisdom*.

Again, let me reiterate the point to follow the Buddha's instructions to the Kalama people that he gave so long ago: test the teachings. At the same time, be prepared to challenge your preconceptions and long-standing habits of mind. These form part of the material we will work with. This takes effort and persistence.

---

2   Sutta (Pali; sutra Sanskrit) – teachings (instructions) attributed to The Buddha.

CHAPTER 1

HOW TO USE THIS BOOK

Cultivating Discriminating Wisdom is one of the most demanding tasks you can ever undertake. It requires that you make sustained effort to see results. We will get brief glimpses of positive results early on. After a year of practice, you may expect to be able to enter the process easily. Maybe a year is not such a long time when you think of the time and effort that goes into getting a university degree. Before you say, "Oh! That is different," who says your long-term psychological and emotional well-being are not worth the effort? Should you have reacted, "Oh! That is different," or reacted in any way at all, please note that was a moment of "What Is Not."

In as much as cultivating *Discriminating Wisdom* is demanding, so is life in general. It makes a difference to take that point into account at the outset. Four major factors set us up to experience life as demanding. These factors are beyond our immediate control. They are conducive to our immediate survival and as adaptation to life 100,000 years ago. They are not conducive to emotional and personal well-being in the complex cultures we have developed. For instance, these factors tend to operate protectively in our psychological reality let alone physical realty. It is one thing to react when a dog is about to attack you. It is entirely another to react angrily at your partner when you have just been accused of not responding to a text.

Overall, our survival is promoted by making quick decisions and acting on them. This strategy is highly efficient but tends to be self-defeating for our longer-term emotional and personal well-being

I wrote above, "These factors are beyond our immediate control." What is within our control is **how we engage with them when they do arise.** For instance, rather than reacting defensively to our partner's accusation, *we would respond by attending to the partner's experience.* This dynamic is addressed in Contrast #10, Ordinary Communication contrasted with *Meaning-Making.*

The four factors are:

Evolution   Your chances of survival were enhanced by anticipating a tiger and realizing it was a delusion rather than assuming you are safe only to be pounced on by a tiger. This genetically endowed caution accounts for what is generally referred to as our "negativity bias." We are generally better off prepared for things to go wrong than to assume they will go right. One major effect is our strong tendency to give far more weight to negative emotions than to positive ones. In turn that contributes to our tendency to define negatively if we have any sense of threat. If that threat is built up in our imaginations, we create a mental habit. We then distress ourselves needlessly so long as we retain the habit.

Neurobiology   From prior to birth onwards, we develop complex patterns of neuronal connections. By five to seven years of age, some key networks have been established in our brains. These connections form patterns of association called "core beliefs" (Contrast #5). These beliefs direct how we relate to world, form relationships, and regard ourselves. We then act on these beliefs. By doing so, we strengthen them and tend to add layers of elaboration over the years. As core beliefs, they can become core delusions. Delusions in the sense that these beliefs bind us into acting in self-defeating ways. This usually happens without us even being aware of what we are doing to ourselves.

Biology in general   Two other key aspects of our biology I want to mention. One is our "natural capacities." The other concerns a few specific hormones, and neurotransmitters. Let us consider each briefly.

1. We are born with an impressive range of "natural capacities" that we never lose. Our capacities to learn, create patterns (these become beliefs and habits), to explore (curiosity), and to initiate action are especially relevant in applying the Contrasts.

    These capacities are useful and necessary. They also contribute to emotional distress in important ways.

However, these capacities get subsumed within our socialization. That is, they function in service of "What Is Not." For instance, think about how young children's curiosity gets constrained by parental figures. An important aspect of learning to live from "What Is" is to be able apply our natural capacities directly, leaving behind self-defeating habits rooted in our socialization.

2. The neurotransmitter Dopamine motivates us to want more and to strive. When the cell phone buzzes, "I've got to answer." We want to take that call; it is the wanting that is rewarding, a moment of anticipation. We then get another shot for taking the call; it is an achievement. We are in control. This function applies widely and was crucial to survival 50,000 years ago. Now seeking these rewards drive dissatisfaction and continued searching.

    Epinephrine (Cortisol) and Norepinephrine (Adrenalin) are key hormones that drive the biologically complex "fight-or-flight" reactions that we experience as emotional distress. That is useful if we are being attacked by a bear. It is dysfunctional when we generate it by imagining, as by worrying or feeling guilty.

    That we react is natural. What we react to and how we react was learned during our socialization. In effect, these are emergency reactions, even though we may not think of the situation as an "emergency." Regardless, these reactions pre-empt our rational capacity to distinguish "What Is" from "What Is Not." We attach to "What Is Not" because believing "What Is Not" generated "the emergency," the distress, in the first place. Our brains justify why we have reacted. Learning to stay in the rationality of "What Is," and releasing ourselves from the power of mental habits, is what this book is about.

Socialization   Throughout our childhoods, we learn from our family "who we are," "who other people are" and how to relate to other people. This set of beliefs and habits form our identity, our "ego." Our ego performs an enormously powerful role in shaping our lives no matter how it is constructed. The derelict on the street has just as demanding an ego as any politician, CEO, or anyone else you might think of.

This combination of evolutionary dictates, neural development and functioning, and our socialization are powerful drivers in our lives. Note the word "drivers." Most accessible of these drivers are the belief systems that run our lives until we take charge. Our beliefs also bind us into living according to "What Is Not." Why this is so will become apparent as you read on.

Practicing *Discriminating Wisdom,* on the other hand, allows us to take charge of our own being. But our egos, supported by evolution and neural patterning, do not want to let go. It takes a great deal of practice to fully take on board that we really have an alternative as well as to learn how to live free of the drivers that have run our lives to date.

Let me reiterate the point: this book is about cultivating peace of mind and a sense of inner freedom. What then might constitute these experiences? Set aside any hope these can be states of being. They are not goals that having achieved them, we remain that way permanently. Rather they are processes we learn to live. In living them, we experience peace of mind and a sense of inner freedom.

At peace, essentially, we feel alert and relaxed even as we attend to what is needed. We accept that events are as they are, and our emotions are appropriate to the situation; they have not been taken over by our ego needs. Likewise, our thinking is smooth, generally reflecting appreciation and present-time awareness. Gone are self-referential concerns, contentious thinking, judgments and so forth. At some point we stop taking life personally, and yet we are fully invested in living.

Let us get a glimpse of the experience of inner freedom. For a start, we sense integrity and are generally able to sustain it. We have embraced living from principles and are no longer driven by desire and aversion. We recognize how we delude ourselves and can readily step out of delusions. We take full responsibility for our choices. We no longer need to defend or justify them. We accept limitations rather than rail against them. This does not imply we simply put up with them.

We will still react against whatever is going on, even as we are laying such a path. Worries still arise, and longing, too. Indeed, the whole gamut of what I will refer to as "ego-involved" thoughts and feelings continue to crop up, although probably with decreasing frequency and severity as we become more skilled in path laying. The main shift is to catch things going amiss sooner and release them with increasing ease. We soon return to feeling at peace and sense inner freedom.

At the beginning of this chapter, I asserted there are four factors beyond our immediate control. However, there is a key aspect that is solely yours. **Namely, you alone can make a conscious and sustained effort to shift out of detrimental habits of thinking and embrace *beneficial* practices. However, you will also resist doing so, and a crucial**

aspect of making the shift is to open to and move through the resistance. One way to help understand these processes is by considering how our brains work (see below and Ch.2).

Most books of a self-help nature include illustrative stories. They have value in certain contexts. Let us call those stories the "content" in that they are illustrating what the author is writing about. However, I am arguing that focusing on content misleads us. This point is examined specifically in Contrast #2, "Content contrasted with *Process*."

In effect, content versus *process* is an issue that underlies much of what troubles us. The issue is that we get caught up in content, principally addressing "what?" and "why?" We generate emotional distress and many of our personal issues by **how we engage,** and that is where this book is focused. *"How?" asks us to examine the processes by which we engage. This is the "What Is!"*

Distinguishing between "content" and "process" risks being experienced as "confusing." This is because talking about parenting, stresses at work, being attached to being on media and having difficulties with one's partner are at one level different topics. At another level, the topic is secondary to how we engage. For instance, the parent who is afraid of being judged by others for their parenting may try to be super-parent. The person who depends on peer approval can be equally driven to respond to every tweet and notification. The underlying psychological dynamics are akin, no matter that they appear different.

In reading this book, please take emotional distress, dissatisfaction, and stress-inducing thinking as signs. They are signs that how you are engaging needs to be examined. An achievement is to examine them with an open mind, self-compassion, and self-forgiveness.

Chapter Two: The Brain – Chapter Two highlights key aspects of neural functioning. Armed with this understanding, we can learn to shift from our normal readiness to engage reactively into a proactive mode of thought. Both are in consciousness, but they represent radically different ways of engaging with our lives moment by moment. Even so, making this shift requires considerable and sustained effort. We need to take it on as life-long practice. Why such effort is required and why we tend to resist is usefully understood in the light of knowledge derived from modern neuroscience.

The subsequent chapters are presented as a series of twenty contrasts. Each Contrast draws attention to an aspect of "What Is Not" contrasted with the alternative perspective of *"What Is."* In introducing the Contrasts here, I want also to show something of the logic underlying the selection of topics and the order in which they are presented.

Each Contrast discusses the "What Is Not" aspect first. *Then we consider "What Is."* **The "What Is" sections are printed in italics in all twenty contrasts.**

Each Contrast ends with suggestions for practice. Indeed, practice is essential if the ideas presented are to make any difference in how you encounter life.

There are far too many practices to undertake them all. One option is to read one Contrast a week and try out the recommended practice over the following six or seven days. In whatever way you chose to read, I suggest you note points you engage with. Review your notes and set priorities to guide how you lay your path as you walk it.

A SPECIAL NOTE ON LANGUAGE AND MEANING

Words matter, but perhaps not in the way we might ordinarily think. We attribute special power and meaning to particular words, gestures, and actions. Their power does not lie in the words themselves but in the meanings we give to those words.

Particular ways in which language or behavior are expressed hook us into our beliefs. These mental associations serve as internal sparks that fire our reactions. I will refer to such gestures as **signs**. Signs are personal; they are unique to the individual. The meaning you give is your meaning. Whatever associations they represent for you are associations that you have generated over time giving them particular personal significance. Signs are usually emotionally loaded. It is language that you identify with. One way or another signs trigger something for you; it can be useful to recognize this as your ego in action. It matters to recognize this is an internal, mental function. **It is not caused by external events**.

Signs are particularly relevant in this book in two ways. The first way is that the examples and practices I suggest may not work for you. This does not mean there is something wrong with the example or the practice. Instead, give the ideas they represent a chance. If an example does not work for you, find an example from your own experience that does fit the idea. Similarly, using particular words I suggest in the practices may not work for you. Find words that matter to you and fit the practice. Words that are meaningful to you are the ones you are likely to work with.

The second way that signs are relevant is in working with our reactivity. Instead of simply reacting, we explore. "What am I reacting to?" Identify the sign. "What does the sign mean to me?" We can make use of each answer to get in touch with our ego-identities and consider what to do next. The Contrasts, outlined in the next section and detailed in the text, consider how we can use diverse ways of engaging to alleviate emotional and personal distress and cultivate benefit.

I have offered many ideas and suggestions in this book. You might react, "This is too much." Rather, read as an explorer. Where do you connect? That is a starting point. Lay down a path from there. Open possibilities from within yourself. This could be the work of a lifetime. May you use your insights for your well-being and for all those whose lives you touch.

TWENTY CONTRASTS

CONTRASTS 1 TO 4

Contrasts 1 to 4 set out basic structures in the ways in which we think that apply to all of us. We use one way of thinking when we live from **"What Is Not,"** which is most of the time. *When we shift to living from "What Is," we use an unusual way of thinking. We become increasingly skilled at handling emotional distress and have the potential to resolve or diminish personal issues that may have existed since childhood – demanding mental and personal work.*

CONTRASTS 5 TO 8 – GOING DEEPER

By now we know what to watch for – defining and being caught up in content, and we can attend to two major barriers – resistance and default mode thinking. We are now ready to go deeper. We explore major, psychological factors bearing upon our thinking in Contrasts 5 to 8.

CONTRASTS 9 TO 20 – TWELVE FACETS OF ONE CORE ISSUE

By this point, we will have discovered how invested we are in our habitual modes of thought and action. A corresponding discovery is realizing just how much effort is required to make the shift. Cultivating peace of mind and finding inner freedom requires dedicated and persistent action – lifelong. The remaining twelve Contrasts offer a range of ways of understanding and attending to making this shift. Working with these Contrasts takes us from encountering life through the lens of "What Is Not" *to living life by engaging with "What Is."*

CLOSING CHAPTER – *"What Then Will You Practice?"*

This chapter reviews the practices suggested in this book. What you choose to practice needs to be "bi-directional." One direction is releasing habits that generate distress. The other is to cultivate benefit, foster peace of mind and realize a sense inner freedom. The test is how we experience the moment. The challenge is to ensure we sustain lifelong practice.

CHAPTER 2

OUR BRAINS – SOME BASICS

OUR GENETIC INHERITANCE

OUR BRAINS – SOME BASICS

Given some understanding of how our brains work and the millions of years of genetic history that makes them function this way, we have achieved three key advances.

We can **learn** to be kinder and more loving towards ourselves (self-acceptance, self-forgiveness).

We can **understand** (1) how to practice shifting from self-distressing thinking to healing thinking, (2) why practice is so demanding and (3) why sustained effort is 100% necessary if we are to keep the shift going. This is a lifetime commitment.

We can **learn** the practices needed to shift from self-distressing, reactive thinking to cultivating our capacities to respond, heal emotionally and achieve a degree of peace of mind and inner freedom.

A diagram of the brain with relevant notes is presented on the next two pages. The diagram shows the Cortex which forms the outer layers covering most the brain (#2 and #3). The Limbic System and Hindbrain (#1) and Corpus Callosum (#4) are represented in cross-section.

OUR BRAINS

BRAIN STRUCTURE (SEE DIAGRAM)

#1 | **Limbic System + "Hindbrain" = "fast brain":** fast reactions, controls bodily/hormonal functions, long-term memory, integrates brain functioning and drives emotions. This is the reactive brain and is discussed below as "The Elephant."

#2 | **Neocortex/Cerebrum** – the outer layers of our brain, highly folded tissue somewhat like the bark of a Douglas Fir.

#3
(a key part of #2) | **Prefrontal Cortex (PFC) = "slow brain,"** together with the Anterior Cingulate Cortex (ACC) and Insular: carries out executive functions, namely: integrating past, present, and future (imagination/creativity), make conceptual distinctions (creates content), allows reflection, makes decisions, manifests personality, and plays key roles in social relations. **The ACC gives us to capacity to initiate and respond intentionally**. Choosing to act intentionally is crucial to making the shift from distressing ways of being towards cultivating peace of mind and a sense of inner freedom. Using this capacity to take charge of our own lives will be referred to metaphorically as "The Driver" below.

The brain has two hemispheres, left and right. The hemispheres have specialized functions. **Left hemisphere:** linear, language, literal, develops relatively later in childhood. **Right hemisphere:** holistic, non-verbal, imagery, metaphors, music.

#4 | **Corpus Callosum** – connects the two hemispheres - thickness varies among people. A key function is to integrate rationality (left hemisphere) with experiential awareness (right hemisphere).

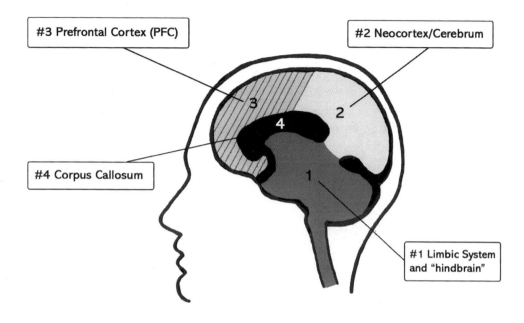

RELEVANCE – WHY UNDERSTANDING THE BRAIN MATTERS

Let me introduce a metaphor to illustrate why understanding the brain matters. The psychologist Jonathan Haidht in his book *The Happiness Hypothesis* describes key regions of the brain as "The Elephant and the Rider." (http://www.happinesshypothesis.com/)

The Elephant is represented by region #1, the limbic system and "hindbrain." These areas are also referred to the "Fast Brain." Region 3, the PFC, is the "Slow Brain," and it functions as "The Rider." These areas are both crucial to our survival and to our sense of well-being, but they get muddled up.

The fast brain is fast. It puts us on alert in somewhere between $^{40}/_{1000's}$ and $^{100}/_{1000's}$ of a second. This includes being highly responsive to Dopamine, as well as Adrenalin and Cortisol. We react. This is the Elephant in action.

The slow brain is *s l o w* – relatively. Response times are a minimum of $^{1}/_{4}$ up to $^{1}/_{2}$ second. That is 10 to 20 times slower than the Fast Brain. This difference in timing means we have already **reacted** before we considered what we are doing. This is great for escaping tigers and bears, and car crashes, but is often a disaster for relationships.

As Elephant, you are acting or reacting in a habitual way. These habits are strongly established and appear to be automatic. As Rider, you have the capacity to consider what to do but can also function out of habit.

As emphasized below, the Rider will characteristically justify reactivity. That is the unwelcome news. The good news is that we can train ourselves to hold off on reacting and give the Rider a chance to take control. The columns compare the difference between **reacting**, the Elephant is in control, and *responding*, the Rider is in control and acts constructively.

Fast Brain – **The Elephant in Charge**	*Slow Brain –* *The Rider in Charge*
Reacting: "Get out of my way!" Anger, fists clenched (for example).	*Responding*: for example, fists clench, "I've tightened right up. I feel so angry. I'm going to take some space."
That is, the Elephant is in control.	That is, the Rider is taking control.
In reaction mode, the Rider's sole job is to justify why the Elephant is doing whatever, no matter what that may be.	**In response mode, the Rider catches reactions;** by recognizing reactivity, you have the capacity to shift to responding
And the Rider **believes** the justification. All too often we fight to defend our justifications.	You, as a skilled Rider, take charge. You know what to do to take care of the situation. For a start, you breathe and relax.
Continuing the example, the Rider now **justifies** by blaming, "You're always telling me what to do. You treat me like I'm an incompetent idiot...!"	Continuing..., the Rider takes responsibility by saying, "I really flared then. I am sorry. Thanks for the space. I still need some time to get really settled. Give me about ten minutes, okay?"
This is enacting "What Is Not." That is, actions are based on belief. Our immediate experience has been buried.	This is staying with "What Is." The Rider's actions are based on being present to both self and other and seeks benefit for both.

THE ELEPHANT IN ACTION

The Elephant in reactive mode (fast brain) goes wherever it wants to – it gets into all kinds of trouble. The job of the Rider is to make sense of why the Elephant is careening through the jungle. The Rider (you) is very clever at finding reasons to justify why the Elephant is cavorting around. Indeed, the Rider is biologically compelled to make sense of the Elephant's actions. This is survival in the jungle.

However, most often our ego is threatened, not our survival. This is where things get muddled up. We still react as if we are physically threatened. Then out come all our justifications, excuses, guilt trips, taking shame and so forth; whatever individual reaction patterns we have developed over the years, and we are totally convinced we are right, at least in the moment.

Being immersed in reacting and being certain about our justifications, we distress ourselves, sometimes intensely. In reacting, all too often we then pull each other into distress and conflict.

Two important points to make about the Elephant and the Rider. First, when we get reactive, the Elephant is in charge. I cannot emphasize that point too strongly. And, at the same time, the Rider **believes** he or she is in charge by justifying. Sorry! No way! The Rider is acting out of habit and is trapped in "What Is Not," for instance believing he is being treated unfairly.

However, with practice, the Rider can learn how to be in charge. The Rider can learn to handle reactions and to respond (See Contrast #11) thoughtfully and constructively. Herein lies the challenge. **This requires you to shift from being caught up in content to practicing with immediate experience (see Contrast #2).** In making this shift, the Rider learns to stay with "What Is" and to practice Discriminating Wisdom.

CHALLENGES IN MAKING THE SHIFT

The shift is challenging for two fundamental reasons. One is "**brain plasticity**," the capacity of our brain to establish new connections. As young children our brains make billions of connections. The brain then operates through those connections as they are established. Each time they fire together, their tendency to fire together is strengthened. This is brain plasticity is action. So, acting out self-distressing habits strengthens those habits.

Add to that the process of identification. We are taught and learn to believe, mostly at an unconscious level, *"who we are,"* what matters to us and why. We do not want to let go of those beliefs. No matter how distressed we get, we have the certainty of knowing who we *believe* ourselves to be. We will go through hell to protect those beliefs.

The skills needed require us to learn to do something different from what our habits, our beliefs, and "common sense" tells us we should do. Fortunately, brain plasticity is with us for life, and we can make use of this capacity to make new connections in our brains by doing the type of practices recommended in this book. In this way, we are perfectly capable of learning the skills required to release both reactivity and distress.

We are equally capable of learning to cultivate our capacities to *respond* constructively and *lovingly* to our immediate experience. Over time, we can cultivate peace of mind and develop a robust sense of inner freedom.

But, and this is a big **BUT**, the skills we need to learn require us to do something different from what our habits and beliefs dictate. This matters in that we defeat ourselves so long as we are in the grip of those habits and beliefs. Making new connections requires effort and lots of practice as well as the persistence needed to off-set the internal resistance that you will encounter.

Let me repeat that point. What I am describing requires a lifetime commitment to effort and practice. If we do not continue to make that effort, our old habits reassert themselves. This happens all too quickly and easily. This point is elaborated in Contrast, #4, Default Mode Thinking – *Making Mental Effort.*

There is no effortless way, no matter what any book promises, or the latest guru tells you. No-one can make the shift for you, and there are no short cuts. But there is guidance and there are signposts. It is your choice. Meanwhile, let us enter the Forest of Contrasts, contrasts between "What Is Not" and "What Is."

CONTRAST #1

DEFINING contrasted with *DESCRIBING*

INTRODUCTION

How we think and speak is a major force in shaping the quality of our lives. We can alter our experience by shifting how we use language. The key distinction is between "defining" and "describing." The next two sections flesh out the difference between definition and description. The subsequent sections highlight why making this distinction matters. The chapter closes with an exercise.

The key is to recognize the role definition plays in shaping the quality of our lives. We define by giving a particular meaning to "whatever." For instance, you were defined as "a boy" or "a girl" at birth and then related to as such. Definition goes on from there. We absorb these definitions and learn to relate to the world and treat ourselves according to those definitions. Key definitions are embedded in our subconscious as beliefs.

Contrasted with defining, we can **describe** *what we observe and experience. "I am feeling so happy to see you again" tells you how I am relating with you experientially in the moment. Description is as close as we can get to expressing our immediate experience verbally.*

How we engage mentally, emotionally, and behaviorally with events makes the difference between becoming emotionally distressed and feeling at ease. Defining, especially as it is expressed in reactivity, tends to lock us into our definitions and contributes to generating further distress.

Description, on the other hand, provides us with opportunities to open to our immediate experience and practice a range of skills that support emotional healing and the cultivation of peace of mind and a sense of inner freedom.

Events – For our purposes, "events" include as any person, actions, objects, any other phenomena, or abstractions that we define.

"WHAT IS NOT" – DEFINING

Words are always about something. They are something other than the experience itself. **Most of the time, we use words to define experience and then continue by further defining our definitions.** We are hooked on our definitions.

Defining minimally categorizes events. From there we elaborate our definitions in many ways. We have, in effect, separated ourselves from our experience.

THE MAIN WAYS WE DEFINE

We will use the following event to exemplify both defining and describing. For example, imagine you react to the phone ringing at lunchtime, annoyed, "What a nuisance!"

Categorization (labeling) – assigns events to a group, a category. Hearing the 'phone is abstracted as a category, "nuisances." We then play out how we, as individuals, deal with this sort of nuisance.

Judgments – assign qualities to events, often based on dualities such as good/bad, right/wrong, or true/false.

"People who phone at mealtimes are inconsiderate (bad)."

Justification – states *why* we feel what we are feeling or *why* we hold a particular opinion. "He should know not to phone at mealtimes. I've told him before."

Opinions – are essentially statements claiming "events" are a certain way or should or should not be that way. Opinions may be voiced about the past, present or an expectation about the future. "People should know better than be on their phones at mealtimes. That's just bad manners."

Stories – are anything we say (or think) about any event (phenomenon) **that gives it meaning**. "Stories" include all the forms of defining listed above, although in some instances "the story" may be incipient. It is not the story itself that makes the difference. Rather it is the meaning we attach to the story that sets up how we act in relation to that story.

A major downside of stories is that all too often we invest our identities in our stories and sacrifice our well-being to them. For example, in talking about my reaction to the 'phone at suppertime, I can exacerbate my initial distress with further justifications, such saying indignantly, "The first time he phoned at lunchtime, I explained to him very clearly I wanted him to call at other times...," and on it goes. This illustration represents the personal perspective. It is important to recognize these processes extend to the broadest reaches of politics and religion.

On the other hand, stories play salient roles in creating a sense of community, connecting us with one another, and in teaching. Contrast #12 looks at this topic in more detail.

While we can identify several ways we define, it is only when we become conscious of what we are doing and how we are doing it that we may choose to shift how we engage with our immediate experience.

"WHAT IS" – THREE WAYS OF DESCRIBING

This comparison is intended to illustrate how we might express our immediate experience in different ways. It is not intended to represent how we might actually speak. How we represent our immediate experience verbally is personal and individual. The key is to be in touch with our experience instead of burying it, for instance, by taking things personally and becoming reactive.

For example, starting with the same initial event: You react to the phone ringing at lunchtime, annoyed, "What a nuisance!"

THREE WAYS OF DESCRIBING

This time, recognizing you are reacting, you shift into descriptive language. Three ways of describing are readily identifiable: sensory experience, meta-cognitive awareness, and planning.

1. **Sensations and thinking** *"I am aware of ...**hearing** ... the phone ringing."*

   seeing *... seeing the plate on the table and glancing up towards the phone.*

   touching *... sense of pressure from having held the plate in my fingers.*

   sensing *... sitting upright; tummy tightening.*

   feelings (emotion) *... uncertain, feeling on the spot.*

2. **Meta-Cognitive Awareness** *(Meta-cognition): "Meta" means "above." "Cognition" is our thoughts and thought processes.* **Meta-cognitive awareness** *then means "looking in*

from above" at your own cognitive processes, being aware of your thoughts. Literally, meta-cognition is thinking about your thinking.

"Wow! Do I ever feel reactive to the phone! I see I am taking it as 'being interrupted'."

*Meta-cognitive awareness includes being aware of our **motivations** and **intentions**. "So, this is the last thing I want to be doing right now, but I'll be friendly." (It is often difficult to be fully in touch with our motivations or even our "real" intentions. Nevertheless, it is worth the effort. Doing so assists us in seeking self-understanding and self-acceptance.)*

This level of awareness permits self-knowledge and self-awareness, and allows us to train our thinking to function constructively replacing earlier self-defeating habits of mind.

3. ***Planning*** *"Planning" involves starting with "What Is," and choosing how to cultivate peace of mind and reduce distress as well as addressing other needs and goals. (Planning is addressed in Contrast #8.)*

"I will explore my sense of being interrupted later. Before I say anything, I need to think about what I am going to say. I want to keep him as a friend and to have calling work for us both. ... "

WHY DEFINING MATTERS

Defining matters because once we have defined a situation, we act in relation to our definition, not to our experience. In this way, the basis for our actions and our thinking depends upon how we construct the situation. We continue by adding further layers of definition. Indeed, we have constructed our reality around "What Is Not." By acting in relation to it, we bring it into being. In this way, "What Is Not" becomes the framework of our lives.

Living from the perspective of "What Is Not" generates an enormous amount of distress for ourselves and other people on an ongoing basis. Defining generates most of our experiences of distress, affecting us personally, our family life, work, and our quality of life in general. I trust you will recognize this as you consider the Contrasts, one by one.

This propensity for defining extends to all forms of strife, for instance, religious and political conflicts. Emotional distress continues until we take charge of our reactive mind, our rambunctious mental Elephant.

On the other hand, we need "What Is Not" both for safety and to organize our lives. We also create a rich diversity of experience within the context our stories. These aspects of "What Is Not" are to be valued. Both sides are discussed in Contrast #10.

Cultivating *Discriminating Wisdom* allows us to stay with "What Is Not" when it is conducive to our overall well-being. On the other hand, we can use this same *Wisdom* to attend directly to our immediate experience, learn to release distress, and cultivate peace of mind and inner freedom.

> **DEFINING MATTERS BECAUSE ONCE WE HAVE DEFINED A SITUATION,**
> **WE ACT IN RELATION TO OUR DEFINITION,**
> **NOT TO OUR IMMEDIATE EXPERIENCE.**

WHY DESCRIBING MATTERS

> *DESCRIBING MATTERS BECAUSE IT ALLOWS US TO RELATE TO*
> *OUR IMMEDIATE EXPERIENCE AND CULTIVATE PEACE OF MIND*
> *AND*
> *A SENSE OF INNER FREEDOM*

When you stay present to "What Is" experientially, you are able to choose how you act, what you do with the meanings (definitions) you generate and how you handle your feelings and emotions. By attending directly to your immediate experiences, notice how you empower yourself to make choices that you otherwise might not have made.

There are two key constraints to description. One is that the language we have available for describing is limited. This becomes obvious when we contrast descriptive language with the rich vocabulary we have available for telling stories. The other is that it requires much more mental effort to describe than to define. Defining adds words to words. To describe as accurately as possible requires us to attend consciously to experience, find language to represent experience and to withhold commentary.

Is it worth it? Do not believe me. Rather, test these ideas out for yourself. If you find them beneficial, practice them – life long. If you find otherwise, search elsewhere. However, keep in mind that we live in a culture that caters to instant gratification. Yet the patterns you have established in your brain have developed since your earliest years. As a reminder, it takes persistence, effort, and compassion for yourself to experience the benefits that accrue by learning to describe in contrast to defining.

Practice #1
Noticing and Naming

For at least a week:

1. **Notice** *getting caught up in stories, opinions etc.*

2. **Name** *what you are doing, "thinking," "arguing," whatever.*

3. **Breathe!** *At least three relaxing breaths, a long breath out letting any sense of stress drain from your body.*

Use reminders *such as flash cards, post-it notes, telephone ringing, kitchen timer, others (?) to get yourself out of the thoughts into noticing.*

Congratulate yourself each time you notice and name what you are doing.

CONTRAST #2

CONTENT contrasted with *PROCESS*

Contrasting "content" and "process" takes us into an entirely different dimension of language from the previous contrast. The two taken together, however, provide the foundation for understanding how we generate emotional distress for ourselves beginning with our mental habits. *Correspondingly, by shifting how we think and speak enables us to cultivate peace of mind and a sense of inner freedom, a life-altering but demanding process.*

Just as much as defining is a dominant aspect of how we ordinarily use language, we also focus on "content," the "what" of what we say. **We usually submerge how we think and speak, namely our "process," how we go about doing anything.** It does not matter whether we are going shopping, having a discussion with a friend, or standing for political office." We tend to get mislead by focussing on content, rather than attending to how we engage.

Certainly, we explicitly consider "process" on specific occasions. We prepare to present a vacation plan to a group of friends, plan to propose to a prospective mate, or prepare to deliver a business report to the board of directors. Overall, however, we pay insufficient attention to "process" and create a lot of distress as we go. This book invites you to focus on process, on how you engage. When the content is focused on an issue, it often gets resolved by engaging in constructive processes.

These foundational concepts can be represented clearly in a 2X2 matrix. These distinctions may not be obvious until we think about them. Perhaps we do not ordinarily consider them because our patterns of speech are largely habitual. However, as we alert ourselves to what we are doing with language, we can learn to use language to reduce distress as well as to cultivate benefit.

Content -----> Process:	Definition	Describing
Skillful: seeking to cultivate benefit	Contrast #10 suggests when we can usefully make use of defining and so work with "What Is Not."	Language conducive to cultivating peace of mind and inner freedom
Unskillful: language generating distress either internally or between people	Forms include worry, judgment, blaming, criticalness, denial, avoidance, the list goes on.	Failure to use meta-cognitive awareness to assert control over thought processes. Failure to plan (see p.18: Planning as a way of Describing).

CONTENT AND PROCESS

I have already suggested that distinguishing between "content" and "process" can be very helpful, and perhaps necessary if we are to truly embrace the idea of laying down a path walking. We need an accurate sense of what we are doing with language to be reasonably assured we are making beneficial choices. Sometimes this is obvious. Screaming at someone out of anger is not skilled. Whereas releasing anger and asserting our needs calmly is more likely to achieve beneficial results.

Ordinarily our use of language is much more subtle. A closer examination of what we do with our language, and how we do it is warranted.

Content	Process
Content is **what** we think about and talk about, examples:	*Process is **how** we bring the content into being and what we do with it, examples:*
The car, cars, houses etc., abstract forms: parliament, the Nation, divorce.	*arguing, agreeing, disagreeing.*
Worries (e.g.: about debts).	*worrying.*
The weather, a war, pandemics, or any ongoing phenomenon.	*advising, criticizing, defending, supporting, undermining.*
Good or bad, right or wrong, moral judgments of any kind.	*holding onto feelings, releasing feelings, acting out, forgiving.*
Opinions about other people, ourselves, relationships, the world.	*promising, threatening, warning, advising, criticizing, manipulating.*
Stories about our families, work, relationships, vacations, the world.	*self-promotion/validation, seeking to impress others, bolstering self-esteem, justifying why you hold a particular opinion.*
Expectations and beliefs.	*working constructively with disappointed expectations. Identifying and releasing self-defeating beliefs.*

Use the following example as a starting point for contrasting "What Is Not" with "What Is."

"I am worrying about paying our mortgage this month."

"WHAT IS NOT" AS CONTENT

There are two points to consider regarding content:

1. Content normally dominates process.

2. Recognize being caught up in content.

CONTENT DOMINATES PROCESS

In the statement ""I am worrying about paying our mortgage this month," the content is "paying our mortgage this month." The conversation could all too easily unfold as an argument, about how on earth do we find enough money to pay the mortgage.

"We've got to take a loan to cover the payment."

"We can't do that. That's so short-sighted!"

And away they go.

Content dominates process largely because defining both conveys a sense of certainty and creates something solid out of the flow of experience. This solidity gives us "material" to work with in our thinking and our behavior.

From the perspectives of evolution (survival) and cognition (energy conservation), we are better off to work quickly with certainties than to be figuring out what is going on. We are also strongly invested in our ego-identities. For example, we usually "know" we are right, or we may "know" we are wrong. Either way, we quickly defend ourselves either asserting our rightness, or perhaps we strive to protect our egos from being wrong. No matter which, we are hooked.

RECOGNIZE BEING CAUGHT UP IN CONTENT

We will always need to talk about the content of our lives. Where this can become problematic for us is when "we are caught up in content." At these times, our mental Elephant is in control. Three straightforward signs of being caught up are:

1. Experiencing distressing feelings, thoughts, and emotions, including feeling (being) self-righteous.

2. Being critical, demanding, or judgmental of others or oneself.

3. Feeling driven to continue or to repeat a story, no matter how brief or how long.

With practice, we can notice being caught up. We become the observer of our own being "caught-up." We are then able to shift to "processing," to attend to whatever has come up for us and especially to practice releasing ourselves from emotional distress. The practices suggested at the end of each Contrast attend to aspects of this shift. Practices #7.1 and #7.2 specifically focus on cultivating equanimity as an alternative to distress.

Return to the earlier example of the couple and the issue of the mortgage. *Assume this couple have already agreed to enter processing when they go off-track. This includes practicing the skills and techniques that support getting back on-track. This perspective is addressed in a number of Contrasts, especially Contrast #12, as well as "processing" in the next section.*

"We've got to take a loan to cover the payment."

"I can feel myself tightening. Let's take this gently and make sure we don't go off-track." They continue processing. When they agree that they are back on-track, they return to discussing how to manage the mortgage payment.

"WHAT IS" – PROCESS

Three points to consider regarding process:

1. *Recognizing process*

2. *Processing*

3. *Shifting how we process*

Recognizing Process – *Recognizing process is a meta-cognitive activity. Start with the Rider taking control by intentionally shifting your focus from "content." Using the example of "paying the mortgage," what are you doing from a process perspective? Perhaps you are worrying.*

"Worrying" and other mental processes are present time experiences. These experiences are independent of the content. Please keep this independence in mind as it is key to understanding the operation of core beliefs (Contrast #5).

Developing our awareness of how we "process" allows us to shift our mental activity away from distressing habits, such as worrying, to beneficial approaches, such as planning (see Contrast #8).

Processing – *The idea of processing is being able to recognize what we are doing by thinking and speaking, recognizing this as patterns. We then release ourselves from self-distressing habits and belief and cultivate benefit through the practice of "Discriminating Wisdom."*

We will attend first to recognizing getting caught up in content (Practice 2.1). Practice #2.2 suggests a next step in processing, "Being 'in truth' with yourself." Contrast #9 explores "truth" in some depth. Meanwhile, keep in mind that **your truth** *is: "representing as accurately as you can your experience in the moment." Your truth does not depend on it being true for anyone else.*

Your truth has less to do with what may be true in the outside world than you might think. For example, you might believe the truth of a religious teaching. Whether or not the teaching is true is independent of the truth of your believing. We can practice being in truth with ourselves by asking questions such as:

- *How are we thinking? "Self-critically," perhaps.*

- *In what role(s) do we cast ourselves? Hero, helpless… . There are many possibilities.*

- *What are our intentions and motivations?*

- *What consequences do we observe?*

- *How are we feeling about what is going on?*

Observing myself, I am able to investigate how I am dealing with the issue of the mortgage, as an example. Here is a beginning:

- *"How am I approaching the mortgage?" "I see I am worrying."*

- *"How am I expressing myself?" "Urgently; with some desperation in my voice."*

- *"What are the consequences of my urgency?" "I sure get myself stressed."*

- *Continue investigating.*

This form of reflection is not difficult to do and yet may well be challenging if it is unfamiliar. Other facets of our psychology also bear on how we engage with self-examination. The remaining Contrasts examine those facets that are most likely to need attention to achieve peace of mind and sense of inner freedom.

Shifting How We Process *– It is one thing to recognize our habits of thought and speech as well as identifying the ones that generate distress. It is quite another matter to adopt self-enhancing ones. As we make this shift, we will notice we are letting go of mental activities that define. Correspondingly, we identify how we are feeling and what we are doing in relation to our feelings, or expectations. We also become increasingly skilled at attending to our feelings and to guiding our thinking in beneficial ways.*

Resistance: *Probably the first boulder to work on is resistance. Our habits of mind are formed liked braided ropes. To the extent you get in touch with your own processes is novel for you, you will be laying down new neural connections. The effort to introduce novelty generally* *feels quite uncomfortable, and we tend to cast doubt to justify not wanting to make the effort. Thoughts like, "I haven't got time" leap in all too easily. Then, our egos usually get in on the act, "Don't tell me what to do!"*

Intention: *A key skill in path laying is to set your intention. "What do you want to achieve in attending to particular mental habits?" Your brain orients to how you state your intention. This makes it a constructive step to frame intentions in a positive form. For instance, suppose you have the habit of being argumentative. Holding the intention to "stop arguing" leaves your brain stuck in a puddle of uncertainty, not knowing which way to go. Shift to a positive intention. "I want to get into empathy with Pat" provides direction. Take "establish positive intentions" as a guiding principle for path laying.*

Exploration: *One key to shifting out of self-distressing modes of thinking into ones conducive to benefit is to become exploratory. Exploring opens our thinking up to novel sets of possibilities.*

Examine your habits and reaction patterns. Find out if working with the suggestions offered in this book, as well as using your own inventiveness, cultivate benefit. Set an intention to become exploratory. Notice when you get reactive. Reflect afterwards. Try out the "processing" questions listed above. What do you discover?

SUMMARY

What we do with language shapes the quality of our lives. No matter what our circumstances, how we render our experience depends on the language we apply. Certainly, we are embedded in our culture, community, and family. What do we make of the current trends? No matter what, some habits of thought generate distress. By revising our thinking and speech, we can shift how we engage with the world, cultivate peace of mind, and experience of inner freedom.

We can shift how we engage with the world by making informed choices about where we invest ourselves in the content of our definitions or, alternatively, practice to release ourselves from emotional distress by modifying how we engage.

The shift occurs differently for different people. Some people start with virtually no self-awareness, although it may not seem like that from within. Other people will have other levels of awareness. On some occasions we can be highly aware. At other times, we are totally absorbed in the drama of our thinking or interaction with other people. Self-awareness has vanished.

As you engage in laying your own path, first expect resistance. Allow that there will be many times you get caught up in content, get reactive or critical, and only realize what happened after the fact.

As you develop self-observation, you come to realize that you are caught up in reacting, for instance, or arguing. As you argue, being aware you are arguing will become more significant than what you are arguing about. You become aware you are distressing yourself in the very moment. You are now able to shift into working constructively with your immediate experience in contrast to continuing to engage in a self-distressing activity.

Persist! Put out "Post-It" notes. You will, with practice, catch yourself earlier and earlier in the process. As you begin noticing reactive feelings arising, you catch them, process both thoughts and feelings, release them and engage constructively, no matter whether this is with your own thinking or whether it is in relating with other people.

With still further practice, you react less and less. You are no longer taking other people personally, and you regard both yourself and the other person or people with respect and compassion.

Over time, you come to experience considerable peace of mind. Increasingly you make choices grounded in caring for yourself as well as other people. You will often find that you meet events with a certain humor, a compassion that recognizes our little parts in, to quote Zorba the Greek, "This whole catastrophe."

Practice #2.1
Recognizing Getting Caught Up in Content

1. *Make a practice of recognizing being caught up in content.*

2. *Reflect on what it was like for you being "caught up."*

3. *Identify the process you are engaged in by naming it, for instance, "trying to persuade," "criticizing," etc.*

4. *Identify how you are feeling emotionally and any associated sensations in your body.*

Note: This practice is intended to both enhance self-awareness and begin the process of laying a path walking by assisting you to cultivate the awareness of "Where you are at" in that moment. Then you figure out the direction you want to take.

Practice #2.2
Processing, Being In Truth With Myself

"What is true to me right now?"

Some more specific questions are:

"What am I doing (mentally)?" "I am... ." e.g.: "exaggerating."

"What am I feeling?" "I am feeling ... ." e.g.: "awkward."

"What am I assuming (believing)?" "I must... ."

"What is my intention?" "

"How do I want to handle this?"

Sometimes we find it difficult to admit our truth to ourselves, let alone other people. Allow that this process is a matter of practice and of bringing compassion and forgiveness to ourselves, step by step.

CONTRAST #3

ENABLING RESISTANCE
contrasted with *OPENING TO RESISTANCE*

Resistance – The sensed experience of "pushing away," from slight to violent. We can say we are resisting when we do not want to hear another person's perspective. Or we do not want to do something that is a departure from what we ordinarily do even though we realize we would likely benefit.

In this book, we are only concerned with resistance in the context of:

1. Resisting releasing self-harming habits of thought and action, such as worrying and putting people down.

2. Resisting cultivating skills and abilities conducive to achieving peace of mind, the experience of inner freedom and relating with others for mutual benefit.

"WHAT IS NOT" – ENABLING RESISTANCE

We enable resistance by defining *the experience of resistance* as something concrete (content) and then acting in terms of the definition, not the experience. Imagine experiencing a moderate sense of resistance at the same time as thinking, "I should meditate, but I don't want to." The thought concretizes "meditation" as content. Reacting to the content strengthens the resistance.

EXPERIENCES OF RESISTANCE MUTATED INTO CONTENT

We can experience resistance in several ways. Not that there is a dramatic difference between them, but being alert to such experiences gives us an opportunity to attend to the resistance rather than get caught up in the content. What constitutes the resistance needs to be identified when it arises.

These examples illustrate the sort of content we might get caught up in:

1. **Distraction** – "Oops. It is time to watch my favorite cartoon," "I must text Peter," etc. Be alert to using "urgencies" as distractions.

2. **Excitement** – "I am so excited about my latest project. Let me see. I want to... ," and "I got so caught up in the project." Is excitement masking attending to something important but less appealing?

3. **Opinions** – holding opinions that prevent you from exploring and, for example, actively cultivating a practice, "Well, there is no proof this works. I am not going to waste my time."

4. **Procrastination** – putting off doing something until later. "I'll do it later!" It may or may not get done later, but if it does, there is some struggle involved in getting it done. If you reschedule and do it as planned without resistance, there is no issue. Be aware of your own patterns.

5. **Rationalization** – apparently logical reasons justifying not doing what you don't want to do, such as "I have too much to do. So... ."

Notice in each instance, the action is in relation to a definition of the situation, not to immediate experience.

"WHAT IS" – OPENING TO RESISTANCE

Opening – to "open" direct your attention to your thoughts, bodily sensations, feelings/emotions, and, possibly, actions and aspects of the environment associated with the experience of resistance; accept them just as you experience them. For instance, imagine thinking, "I should meditate, but I don't want to." At the same time, you experience a moderate sense of "pushing away." Staying with the "What Is" of your immediate experience, I will illustrate opening to resistance using the forms of resistance listed above.

OPENING TO RESISTANCE

1. *Opening to distraction* – *"Oops. It is time to watch my favorite cartoon. I can always practice later. Oops, I see I am resisting practicing." Continue with Practice #3.*

2. *Opening to excitement* – *"I am so excited about my latest project. Wait a moment. Let me sense that... . I sense that energy; I'm almost quivering." Continue with Practice #3.*

3. *Opening to opinions* – *Noticing the thought, for example, "Well, there is no proof this works. I am not going to waste my time. Wait a minute ... (breathe. See Practice #3)." "Maybe there is no proof. No matter. I want to explore how come I jump into that pit!" (Contrast #5 addresses "exploring.")*

4. *Opening to procrastination* – *Noticing the thought, "I'll do it later!" "Wait a minute. I'm wanting to put it off and I don't come back to things. Let me get in touch with that...." Continue with Practice #3.*

5. *Opening to rationalization* – *Noticing the thought, "I have so much to do." "Ah! Caught it! I am justifying not meditating. I can let that go." Continue with Practice #3.*

MORE ON RESISTANCE

Earlier I wrote, "these examples **understate** resistance." Even using the word "understate" **understates the power of our minds.** This is because resistance represents the resilience of our habitual modes of thought. These habits militate against actually resolving the many ways in which we generate emotional distress for ourselves.

We have to be willing to encounter our resistance and release it if we are to cultivate peace of mind and inner freedom. It does not matter how many books we read, how many teachers we go to or how many practices we undertake, it makes no substantial difference so long as we sustain our habitual ways of thinking and encounter life through a lens of beliefs. These beliefs are ones we incorporated preconsciously during our childhoods to adapt, primarily, to the family in which we grew up (See: Contrast #5).

First, however, we have to be prepared to take on resistance, irrespective of how it shows up. Resistance comes into play as soon as we try to reform our mental habits. Indeed, these habits operate as the **default setting** for our brains. We default to habitual patterns of thought when we do not deliberately focus on a task.

Recall the metaphor of the Rider and the Elephant. Our default is to have the Elephant in charge. It takes considerable mental effort for the Rider to assert control over the Elephant. Making the shift from default thinking to making mental effort helps us move through resistance and to open to other features of mental operation. The next Contrast examines this issue.

BE AWARE

*RELEASING RESISTANCE IS A CRUCIAL STEP
TO CULTIVATING PEACE OF MIND AND A SENSE OF INNER FREEDOM.*

LEAVING RESISTANCE OPERATING SUSTAINS WHATEVER MENTAL HABITS
YOU HAVE ACQUIRED OVER YOUR LIFETIME THAT GENERATE DISTRESS.

Practice #3
Processing resistance*

1. *Sense the "pushing away," your sense of wanting to avoid, dismiss, reject, or deny.*

2. *Accept, "This is exactly how I feel …(the pushing-away)."*

3. *Either breathe in the sense of "resisting," Or, name the type of thought, for example "Justifying (why I don't want to do it!)."*

4. *Breath out the thought, "Let it go," relaxing your body on the out breath.*

5. *Repeat #3 and #4 until the resistance dissipates and you can enter the practice or activity you were resisting.*

This is a gentle process of allowing yourself to engage, not trying to force yourself to do so.

* This practice is based on the ancient Tibetan practice of Tonglen.

CONTRAST #4

DEFAULT THINKING contrasted with
MAKING MENTAL EFFORT

DEFAULT THINKING

From about middle childhood on, we develop patterned ways of thinking. Subsequently, our brains default to specific patterns when we are not task focused. For instance, I am mowing the lawn. Halfway through I find I am deeply worried about something; it has nothing to do with mowing. Worrying is one of my default modes. I now recognize that this one is telling me that I am bored. On the other hand, if I am engaged in figuring out a sudoku puzzle, I am engaged in a task. No such worrying occurs.

The idea of "default thinking" goes along with recent findings in neuroscience. We now understand how our brains flip into a particular form of brain connectivity, called the "default mode network," when we are not engaged in attending to tasks. In default mode, we think about the past and the future, about ourselves, and about other people. As we will see in a moment, we can make use of these experiences *to recognize when we are engaged in default mode thinking.*

At least some modes of default thinking appear to be harmless, such as daydreaming. On the other hand, distress is generated by a number of default modes. Worrying, thinking critically and mentally generating anger are three prominent examples. This is the Elephant on a rampage; the Rider just gets bounced around.

This contrast draws attention to modes of default thinking that are associated with the distress. While we may be aware we have these habits, we tend to take them as givens, as if we do not have any alternative available to us. The point of this contrast is to offer an alternative that releases distress. However, achieving release requires us to make mental effort. Effort is needed to counter the power of mental habits. Then, recognizing we are in "default mode," we can go deeper. This is discussed as Contrast #5, which addresses beliefs that fire up default thinking and self-distressing ways of being in the first place.

MAKING MENTAL EFFORT

Whatever your distressing defaults may be, you will have identified with them. They are part of your Elephant, and you can be sure it is a powerful beast to tame. Take worrying as an example. The logic in our subconscious could operate something like this: I identify myself as a conscientious person and worrying is a sign to me that I am being conscientious. Not worrying would signal to me that I am not really conscientious. I will not accept that. I am better off with the distress of worrying."

By paying attention, we come to recognize that we are caught in a distress-generating belief system. It requires mental effort to learn and practice a beneficial alternative. Making this shift demands a lot of us. Part of this demand is that we are actually developing new synaptic connections in the process of learning. Initially, these connections are very weak and are easily over-ridden by habitual modes of thought. Ongoing practice is necessary to sustain the shift.

The combination of resistance, wanting to hang onto our identifications, and the effort to form new connections explains why, as Riders, we have to make substantial and conscious mental effort to get our brains to learn a constructive way to operate. This, indeed, is the Rider taking control.

Let me emphasize these points. Notice that default thinking wells up easily in your mind; you do not have to make conscious effort for it to occur. Making mental effort is the opposite. This effort is exactly what takes your brain out of a default mode network and into task function. Instead of doing the default thinking, *the default thinking itself becomes the subject of what you are doing. It is the "What Is."* We choose particular modes of thought and enact them deliberately. The section "What Is" – "Making Mental Effort" provides suggestions for how to go about this task.

"WHAT IS NOT" – DEFAULT THINKING

Default thinking is dwelling in "What Is Not." We define what is going on by telling ourselves a story. All too frequently we distress ourselves with the stories we are telling ourselves. We do so in a number of ways.

Avoidance and Denial are indicated by excuses and rationalizations for not considering what is difficult for us to face. We may or may not be aware we are justifying our behavior. We protect ourselves from being aware of how strongly we climb into our stories. As examples, anger and blaming are often useful indicators of avoidance and denial.

Criticalness and Self-righteousness assume the right or need to judge. Look to see if only your perspective counts (sole judge). Other people are seen as failing in one way or another. Notice if you are assuming you are right, perhaps with some sense of superiority in your perspective.

Defensiveness and Reactivity indicate one or more significant beliefs about yourself is being invalidated, such that your meaningfulness as a person is being questioned. Perhaps this will be by the actions of another person; certainly it is being undermined by your own belief system.

"Drivenness" can be identified in your body as sensation and may be experienced as "pressure," or you may feel a sense of "urgency." Likewise, you may have a thought like, "I must do... ." Note how you will usually come up with good reasons as to why you "must do it." The "it" ranges from "must" answer the cell phone to "must" get promoted at work (see: "Fast Brain" pp.11-12).

Negativity is encountering life through a lens of "What is wrong" and/or "What could be improved." This is not to say that everything is actually okay. Much needs attention, such as the car not performing well or someone's criticalness. That is content and is usefully treated separately. We are concerned here with a mindset that generates ongoing dissatisfaction and distress. However, this mind set also conveys egocentric gains, such as "being superior," or "knowing better."

Worry is mentally doing something to deal with difficulties. How connected the worry might be with external circumstances varies widely. No matter what the connection might be, mental power is such that we react physiologically. Bodily sensations and feelings give us the illusion that we are actually doing something about the situation. With that sense operating pre-consciously, we can really climb into the worry and become highly distressed. Indeed, you may even experience greater distress worrying than if you encountered the initial situation in real life.

"WHAT IS" – MAKING MENTAL EFFORT

"Making mental effort" attends directly to default thinking. In doing so, we are dealing with the "What Is" of the default experience. The mental effort is us intentionally training the Rider to take control by noticing and intervening when default thinking is operating.

1. *Identify* and **Name** the type of default thinking occurring, preferably as it occurs. Recognizing in hindsight heads you in the right direction (c.f.: Practice #1).

2. **Accept** – *"Yes, this is what I am doing."* No blame; no judgments; no justifications; no stories (Practice #2.1 & 2.2),

3. **Making Mental Effort** – letting go of default thinking and engaging in an intentional mental task that brings you, that is your thinking and awareness into present time (see Practice #4, below). Such effort is made both consciously and intentionally.

Avoidance/denial: Notice, name and accept "justifying." "What am I trying to protect myself from?" We need to take courage to acknowledge "the unacceptable " about ourselves and/or our situation.

Criticalness/Self-righteousness: Notice and name "judging." Notice assuming the right or need to judge. Look to see if only your perspective counts. What you believe will appear to you as being right, good, true, or fair.

Defensiveness/Reactivity: Notice and name "hooked." If the name "hooked" does not work for you, find an alternative, such as "trapped" or "hurt."

Drivenness: Drivenness can be identified as sensation in our bodies. It is often experienced as pressure, or a sense, "I must do...," or one of "urgency." Note how we come up with good reasons why we "must do 'it'," "It" ranges from must answer our cell phone to must climb the corporate ladder. Notice sensations.

Negativity: Notice and name, such as "finding fault," or noticing "but... ." Name it, "But." A few other clues of negativity are, "If only... ," "It would better if... ," and "This is worse than... ."

Worry: Notice and name, "Worrying." Ask yourself, "What am I trying to do? What am I trying to be?" Here you are investigating the function of worrying; you are not trying to solve the problem represented by the content of the worry.

Practice #4
Making Mental Effort

There are a number of ways to switch from default thinking to a task-focused mode of thought. One such practice follows. Focused mental effort is needed in order to cultivate beneficial thought in place of habitual self-distressing thinking.

Use this practice as soon as you notice you are in default mode. Repeat as thought or say aloud (circumstances permitting) as many times and with as much mental intensity as you need in order to release yourself from the grip of default thinking.

1. Repeat "Let it go. Let it go. Let it go. ... ."

2. Use a mantra, "Om mani padme hum" or a blessing, "May I be well. May I be happy. May I be at peace" or any word(s) you chose that require intentional thought (This is "The Rider" taking control),

3. Ground in the present. Look around and name what you see.

4. When you feel grounded and ready to proceed, start by planning how you will proceed.

All the while practice relaxing breathing: take a deep breath in and relax with a longer breath out. Let your muscles relax throughout your body

Return to your choice of options 1 through 3 any time default thinking associated with mental and emotional distress reasserts itself. Allow that this is a demanding practice. Your Elephant is willful.

CONTRAST #5

CORE BELIEFS contrasted with *EXPLORATION*

"Core beliefs" are the Elephant that runs our lives until we, as the Rider, take control. We gain control by identifying and exploring these beliefs whilst they are operating. First, we will consider the idea of belief in general and then discuss core beliefs, as "What Is Not," and lastly the "What Is" of exploration.

Belief is such a powerful force in our lives. Beliefs define how we live and shape the quality of our lives. For the most part they operate subconsciously. From the perspective of our brains, a key neurological function of belief is to make associations. These associations are literally formed in neural connections in the brain. An example of a relatively insignificant belief could be that I believe that butter is bad for my health, but a little butter is okay. Someone else's belief could be such that they will not consume any animal fats whatsoever. On the other hand, if as a child I learned to associate tension in my tummy with something being wrong externally, then as an adult I may be particularly prone to noticing things wrong around me. In construing something wrong, my tummy will tighten confirming there is something wrong. I act on that construction, the "What Is Not" of defining the situation as something wrong and create a self-fulfilling prophecy.

All that we know and the ways in which we know (e.g., skeptically, optimistically, etc.) are built on structures of belief. Many are necessary and entirely functional. However, for those beliefs to function they, too, need to be organized. These organizing beliefs can be understood as "core beliefs." There are only certain core beliefs that we need to attend to here. These are the ones that drive our quality of life. In particular, we are concerned with identifying those that cause distress in our lives.

"WHAT IS NOT" – CORE BELIEFS

Core beliefs define the way we relate to life. They developed unconsciously in our minds by the time we were five or so. We seem to acquire two to four such beliefs. Our core beliefs form as strongly connected neural pathways when, as children, we were adapting to emotionally challenging family patterns and traumatic events.

Once core beliefs are formed, everything else **that is personal** gets organized in relation to them. Operating unconsciously, they set us up to carry their effects into adulthood. It bears repeating that core beliefs define how we relate to events, and we then act according to the "What Is Not" of that definition. For instance, it is only through the filter of core beliefs that we take other people's behavior personally. We react with anger, for instance, depending upon how we defined their behavior in the first place.

Core beliefs have two main effects on us as adults. One is that they define our ego-identities and constrain how we view ourselves and relate to other people. This is especially relevant in intimate relationships. The second effect is to drive us to behave in certain ways, such as to be jealous, to work all the time, to be negative, or perfectionistic.

We can understand how core beliefs operate by imagining that our parents and other emotionally significant people put glasses on us. The glasses work so that we learned to see life from their point of view and learned about ourselves through their eyes. As children we do not know this is happening. At the same time, it is unavoidable. Core beliefs operate in ways that prevent us from recognizing that we are wearing the glasses in the first place, and they ensure that we experience distress in at least some areas of our lives.

> **Core beliefs have two main effects on us as adults: They define our ego-identities and, constrain how we view ourselves and relate to other people. They drive us to behave in certain ways, as in being judgmental or to over-expect.**

Here, we will work with a list of six common core beliefs. They operate as dimensions with contrasting poles, e.g.: good — bad. Depending on how we were socialized and how we adapted to that socialization, we will structure our lives accordingly. The examples given with each dimension illustrate how that dimension might operate in your life. Start with a "ballpark" idea for your core beliefs then you can refine how you name them using language that is meaningful to you.

Core Issues	Examples of Beliefs
Dimensions of Belief	What **beliefs** do you identify with? Or find equivalents that work for you. Look for 2 to 4 that resonate; make a note of them.
Morality Good – Bad Right – Wrong Better – Worse	"I must prove I am good." "I am bad." "I must fight the good fight." "I must fight against… (add in)." "I am on the side of justice." "I know what is right." Shame and guilt are often recurrent experiences. Core beliefs underly guilt and shame. It is core beliefs that trigger this type of experience, not associated events.
Power I matter – I don't matter Important – Nothing Strong – Weak ("Power" in the sense of personal power.)	"I must prove I matter." "I fear I don't matter." "I must prove I am important." "I am nothing." "I am strong." "I fear being seen as weak." "I never do quite as well as I might." "If I speak up, I am going to get stomped on, or worse." "I can always do better." "I do my best." "I am independent." "I am ashamed of myself."
Truth True – False Honest – Dishonest	"I know." "I am right (e.g., my opinions are the correct view)." "I must prove I am right." "I know the other person is wrong." "I am honest."
Desirability Lovable – Unlovable Attractive – Unattractive	"I am lovable." "I must prove I am lovable." "I feel unlovable." "Nobody truly loves me." "I must look my best." "I need to be seen as attractive." "I am attractive." "I am not attractive."
Safety Safe – Unsafe Trust – Mistrust	**Note:** A sense of being safe is ordinarily independent of immediate situation. "I am not safe." "I don't (can't) trust other people."
Personal Value Valuable – Worthless	**Note:** Personal value is likely to be associated with Power and/or Desirability. "I deserve." "I don't have anything to offer." "I must please others." "I need to be the center of attention." "I don't want to be noticed." "If it is easy, I am not trying." "I must always do my best."

Core beliefs set us up for a lot of difficulties. Much of the time, especially in intimate relationships, we feel compelled to prove our beliefs or to prove that our partner is wrong or is against us. We can all too easily delude ourselves that our reactivity means there is something wrong with our partner or with ourselves. Maybe we see it as our lot in life to be martyrs or victims. Maybe we have to play the hero. Or, again, we may deny or avoid taking any responsibility for attending to the demanding aspects of core beliefs.

Our core beliefs run our lives until we take charge. Ordinarily we focus on **"content."** Content is the *"what"* of what we are concerned about. As examples: **what** *we worry about* (bills, perhaps). **What** *we are angry about* (a relationship?). **What** *we feel hurt or ashamed of* (for example: being criticized). Meanwhile we are not aware that **how we engage** with the content is shaped by our core beliefs.

Core beliefs have many **feelings, thoughts, stories, memories,** and other, **secondary beliefs** associated with them. These are formed as patterns in our brains. This is why we **react** in quite repetitive ways to particular sorts of events. Our reactions focus on the content, and by focusing on the content we then strengthen its significance in our brains. We experience content, core beliefs, thoughts, and reactions as a self-reinforcing loop.

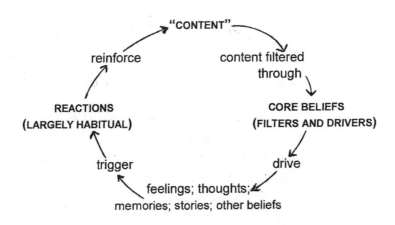

An example of core beliefs operating is if you feel compelled to answer a cell phone, or, correspondingly, an urge to text your friend or partner. That sense of compulsion or urge comes essentially from a combination of a core belief operating and a surge of dopamine. The dopamine energizes you and the core belief shapes the story you will attach to the urge. If you look at the story, ordinarily you will probably find it operates both as justification and an explanation for why you acted in a particular way. I will give a few instances to illustrate this process. Please do not take them as being diagnostic; they merely represent very few of many possibilities.

Rolf has a core belief that he only matters if other people approve him. The phone rings. He has got to answer, or risk disapproval. The felt sense of "got to... " illustrates the urge I am referring to.

Melynda has a core belief that she must be caring. Not to answer the phone would demonstrate that she is uncaring.

Sammy's core belief is that he is not worthwhile, and that he is going to be abandoned. Celia doesn't text back. Over the next couple of hours at work, he builds up a rather panicky sense of desperation. By the time he gets home, he is storming angry.... .

Suzie questions her own lovability. Getting texts from Amin hold her fears at bay, for a short while anyway. If she texts him first, then in her belief system he only replies because he feels obligated to do so, and that is a sign she is not lovable.

In summary, what I have described is the "What Is Not" of beliefs. Again, this is "What Is Not" because we act on the basis of our beliefs about the situation, not our immediate experience of the situation. In doing so we reinforce and perpetuate whatever loops of distress we have developed over our lifetimes.

It is important for you to recognize that:

Your belief system controls the quality of your life, not the content!

Beliefs are powerful drivers in our lives. Some people can identify and work with their own core beliefs. For many people finding a counsellor who is able to assist them in working directly with core beliefs is probably advisable.

WHAT IS – EXPLORATION

*In order to explore, we set content aside for the moment. "Content" represents **issues** that need attention one way or another **(see Contrast #6)**. First, we attend to the emotionality and reactivity associated with the operation of core beliefs. With practice, we learn to keep ourselves out of the cycle, illustrated opposite, in which the Elephant is running the show. We learn to cultivate our sense of autonomy instead. This sense is cultivated by making choices for ourselves and taking responsibility for those choices. Think in terms of making choices that* are conducive to our longer-term well-being. This is the Rider taking control of the Elephant. While the Elephant is still there, you are practicing and, over time, you tame it.

Exploration takes us into the immediate experience of the operation of core belief. In Contrasts #1 to #4, I recommended the practice of Noticing, Naming, Accepting, and Releasing. Start by applying that same sequence in working with core beliefs and add "Exploration."

The following recommendations are intended, first, to assist in identifying core beliefs, and second, to assist in working with core beliefs as you become aware of them.

IDENTIFYING CORE BELIEFS

1. **Noticing core beliefs operating** – Notice taking other people personally, taking offense, being reactive and feeling defensive. Be aware of default modes of thought, such as repeatedly doubting your decisions, also feelings such as feeling driven. These experiences are generated through the operation of core beliefs.

2. **Breathe** – Give yourself time to explore what is going on for you in respect to core beliefs. Take relaxing breaths. Allow that taking care of your well-being matters to you.

3. **Identifying a core belief** – Ask yourself the question "What must I believe about myself to react like that?" Allow an answer to bubble up in your mind. The answer may feel uncomfortable; something that we may well not want to recognize in ourselves and yet need to if we are to get past self-distress.

4. **Acceptance** – Practice acceptance. "This is what is true for me right now." This is exactly how it is for you at this point in time. No more; no less. No judgment, no justifications, no story. If you find yourself resisting accepting, then that is what is true for you in the moment. Offer yourself a blessing, "May I accept that 'this core belief' seems to be operating."

ALLEVIATING THE POWER OF CORE BELIEFS

As we become able to recognize core beliefs operating, it becomes a matter of noticing at the time. You may find that this recognition comes after the episode is well over. It is progress just to recognize our core beliefs at work. With practice, you will become quicker at recognizing the experience.

1. **Notice and Name the core belief** – Notice what indicates that a core belief is operating, e.g., defensiveness, reactivity in general. "Name" the core belief. One useful way of phrasing the name is as a "need" expressed from an observer perspective. If I think of myself reacting to being taken for granted, I observe, "I see I need to matter. I take what she just did as a sign that I don't!"

2. **Breathe and Accept** – *Breathe into the distress. Breathe out relaxing breaths. Notice changing sensations in your body. Practice acceptance. "This is what is true for me right now." If you encounter resistance to accepting, "May I accept that 'this core belief' (e.g.: "I'm not good enough") is operating."*

3. **Exploration** – *is a matter of developing self-awareness and self-knowledge. Apply only one or two questions to aid your exploration. Otherwise, the range of possibilities could prove overwhelming and deter pursuit of learning about yourself. Here are a range of exploratory questions. Please feel free to get creative.*

   - *"How is this belief **effecting** me?" Example: "I mustn't trust," Effect: "I must be on guard all the time."*

   - *What **role** does this belief allow me to play in my imagination? And in my life? Example: "I must matter." Role: I strive to be "the hero."*

   - *What do I **gain** through this belief? Or what **need** gets addressed through this belief? Look for aspects of personal meaningfulness and/or confirmation of the belief. Example: "That proves I'm a loser." Gain: I don't have to take a risk. Is there a **fear** operating? Imagine you did not do what the belief demands and allow any feared consequences to well up in your mind. Example, "If I didn't please Mom, what would happen?" "She'd be mad at me."*

   - *What **triggers** this belief? When is it not in operation?*

   - *Ask yourself, "Why does this belief matter to me? Why is it important?" Apply the same question to the answer with the goal of homing in on your core belief. Example: "Why <u>must</u> I try hard?" "That shows I am conscientious." "Why does being conscientious matter to me?" "That proves I'm important." Bingo!*

   - *Beliefs have their own **internal logic**. That is, belief may well not appear "logical" to an external observer or even to ourselves! But if we can follow their logic, they are ironclad powerful. This internal logic binds us into our beliefs. Explore by asking, "What is the logic connecting these ideas?"*

   - *Look for "**If – Then**" logic. Example: "**If** I didn't please Mom, what would happen?"*

   - ***Then**, "She'd be mad at me."*

   - *Look for "**Either – Or**" logic. Example: "**Either** I work all the time, **or** I'll go bankrupt."*

Let us now apply these ideas briefly to the four illustrative examples used in the previous section. These examples also demonstrate the practice suggested for working with core beliefs, Practice #5, below.

Rolf has a core belief he only matters if other people approve of him. The phone rings. He has got to answer, or risk disapproval.

Rolf: "There's that urge to answer. Again! I need approval so strongly." Rolf breathes, relaxes and explores; it is familiar territory. "May I forgive myself for being so scared. Let me allow the possibility the caller will not be condemning." Rolf lets the fear-inducing fantasy go. "I choose not to answer. I will attend to any consequences should they arise." Rolf is staying present time.

Melynda has a core belief she must be caring. Not to answer the phone would demonstrate that she is uncaring.

Melynda: "I am swamped. I can't answer. I must. What is going on here? Maybe I should try that core belief thing. What must I believe to think I've got to answer? Oh! Wow! I'm not caring ... I've got to be. Maybe there is something to this core belief stuff ... ."

Sammy's core belief is that he is not worthwhile, and that he is going to be abandoned. Celia doesn't text back. Over the next couple of hours at work, he builds up a rather panicky sense of desperation. By the time he gets home, he is storming angry.... .

That was last time – two weeks ago. Celia had made it clear to him. Their relationship is on the line. *Sammy got into counselling quickly!*

Sammy is at work. Celia didn't text back. It's 3 p.m. Sammy notices tension in his stomach and his head start on a story about Celia. *Sammy: "Tension! There's that not worthwhile story! Breathe." "Wow! I actually feel less tense. (Explores) I see now how I am pulling myself down. May I forgive myself. 'I don't deserve it' Ow! Where did that come from? More work to do."*

Suzie questions her own lovability. Getting texts from Amin hold her fears at bay, for a short while anyway. If she texts him first, then in her belief system he only replies because he feels obligated to do so. She takes this as a sign that she is not lovable.

Suzie texted Amin ... again! And, again, with no reply. *Now Suzie is in tune with her core. Indeed, she is quite advanced in her practice.*

Suzie to herself: "Ugg! That was a sharp tightening. I looked at my phone. Seems so innocuous but it sure is loaded; a powerful sign ("Signs" are discussed on p.6). Breathe. I do not need to judge my lovability any longer. May I let it go."

CONCLUSION

Getting in touch with core beliefs can be especially challenging. We usually like to think that we are in charge of how we conduct ourselves. Certainly, at one level most of us have some measure of control over our lives. To the extent we experience emotional distress, pervasive seriousness, a sense of drivenness, defensiveness and so forth, core beliefs are in control, not us. By "not us" I mean in the sense of exercising autonomy, our capacity to make choices and release psychological and emotional constraints.

In taking on working with core beliefs, we invest time, energy, and specific practices. We may well wonder if it is worthwhile. It is an act of faith to make this investment, as it is with financial investments. In this instance, at least, the return on our investment depends on our commitment and effort. Working with core beliefs provides us with a short cut to working with a key psychological "mechanism," one that accounts for our experiences of emotional distress.

Practices #5.1 and #5.2 are abbreviated versions of the text above. Should you want to review details, please refer to the text.

Practice #5.1
Identifying Core Beliefs

1. <u>Notice core belief operating</u> Notice reactivity. Notice sensations in your body, including urges or the sense of drivenness.

2. <u>Breathe</u> Give yourself time to explore what is going on for you in respect to core beliefs. Take relaxing breaths. Allow that taking care of your well-being matters to you.

3. <u>Identify the core belief</u>.. Either using the list given earlier (p.43) or ask yourself the question "What must I believe about myself to react like that?"

4. <u>Acceptance</u> Practice acceptance. "This is what is true for me right now." Offer yourself a blessing, "May I accept that 'this core belief' seems to be operating."

Practice #5.2
Alleviating the Power of Core Beliefs

1. <u>*Notice and Name the core belief*</u> *Notice what is indicating that a core belief is operating, e.g., defensiveness, reactivity in general. "Name" the core belief.*

2. <u>*Breathe and Accept*</u> *Breathe into the distress. Breathe out relaxing breaths. Notice changing sensations in your body. Practice acceptance: "This is what is true for me right now." If you encounter resistance to accepting, "May I accept that 'this core belief' is operating."*

3. <u>*Explore*</u> *the operation of the belief so as to alleviate its power over time. Apply one or a few questions from p.47. Feel free to get creative.*

4. <u>*Cultivate Autonomy*</u> *Recognize the gain(s), risk(s), fear(s) and/or role(s) entailed in the belief. Explore the choices you can make. What can you choose to do right now that is conducive to your well-being?*

You may find your thinking is self-punitive (undermining choosing). In this case, consider practicing self-forgiveness (see: Contrast #20).

CONTRAST #6

EGO-INVOLVEMENT contrasted with *BECOMING FREE*

"WHAT IS NOT" – THE EGO AND EGO-INVOLVEMENT

Take **ego** to stand for a deeply held system of beliefs that maintains the sense of "I," "me," and "mine." This language represents our being separate from everything that "I" define as "not me." It is essential that we maintain separateness for survival and day-to-day functioning. Doing so in itself is not problematic. However, we get into trouble by becoming ego-involved, in needing to protect or assert some belief about ourselves or the world in matters ranging far beyond basic survival. We benefit by recognizing when being ego-involved is detrimental to both our short-term and long-term well-being, and then release those attachments.

We will first consider the constitution of ego. Next, we will attend to ego-attachment. Finally, we will address ego-involvement.

EGO/EGO-IDENTITY

It is typically easy to recognize elements of our ego-identifications. For instance, you respond when your name is called. Many people react when their name is misspoken. For instance, being called "Dave" by my boss when it matters to me to be called, "David" can really get my blood boiling. That may seem like a minor example of identification, but it is important to recognize sometimes we can attach powerful meanings to "minor" events. Are you ever in trouble for looking at your cell phone while talking to someone else? At the other extreme are the lengths that people will go to assert their importance, for example bosses who bully and use anger to get their way, or the assumption of rightness adopted by fundamentalist religious teachers.

Each person constructs a wide-ranging system of identifications over their lifetime. I use the word "system" intentionally to imply that one way or another these identifications are interrelated. While they tie into core beliefs, they also extend far beyond. This extension is why we can be upset when we are faced with a lengthy line up at the supermarket. Generally, we do not recognize any association with our core beliefs or even with our beliefs overall. We seem more likely to attribute any distress to having to wait, not our construction of this particular period. After all, we could meditate.

In a sense it is beyond us to recognize all or even most of the nature of our individual egos, but we can easily recognize it when it is in action. Think of ego as a large parasite. This parasite clings tenaciously to your back, dug in behind your left shoulder. (Why the left? Latin for left is *sinister,* and "sinister" characterizes ego well.) The ego-parasite feeds on pride, self-righteousness, anger (yummy), embarrassment, hurt, jealousy and resentment, and it feasts on worry. This list is only the beginning. However, *when we shift to "What Is" we can turn these negatives into manure for cultivating inner freedom.*

Should that description of ego appear harsh or judgmental that is not my intent. Rather this Contrast is intended to address a psychological process through which we generate distress for ourselves and dissension with other people when but for our egos there could be connection.

EGO-ATTACHMENT

"Ego-attachment" refers to the specific beliefs and meanings that constitute our ego-identities. Attachment is our relationship with content; it is how we maintain a separate sense of "I," "me" and "mine." As we become attuned to ourselves, we become aware of what we are attached to. Once recognized, we can investigate the attachment, practice releasing it and stop feeding the ego-parasite.

It can be helpful to recognize that we usually only assert or react to our attachments under quite specific conditions. As a general example, we may be overly attached and distressed at home and in our work life but go away on holiday and all that stuff falls away. You may say, "Oh, of course. You're on holiday." If you are willing to explore ego-involvement, you will find that if you are fully enjoying your vacation, you left your parasite behind. But if you feel dissatisfied, you brought it with you. Ego gets idiosyncratic when we look for more specific examples because each of us has a unique set of "sensitivities." Anything you take personally counts. If the cashier at the supermarket is cold or unfriendly, one customer will believe he, the customer, has upset the cashier. For another, the cashier is probably having a difficult day, and he offers understanding.

As mentioned, the attachments that form our ego-identity are wide-ranging. Here is a limited list of examples: **Roles** – being the boss, underdog, or victim. **Community** – identified with nationality, religion, education level, political persuasion, philosophy. **Physical** – health, foods consumed, exercise, appearance. **Interests** – hobbies (the garden!), playing cards, cell phone or Facebook. And Wow! The list goes on and on. Both of the following quotes are attributed to Socrates: "Know thyself" and "The unreflective life is not worth living." Both are worth reflecting upon in the context of this contrast.

This is not to say that all ego-identity is wrong, bad, or detrimental to us. Even someone who is wholeheartedly committed to releasing ego-attachment is still probably going to get hooked on their own opinions. *Keep those attachments that contribute to well-being; release those that generate distress and cultivate the wisdom to know the difference.*

EGO-INVOLVMENT

Take **ego-involvement** to indicate the expression of being ego-attached. It serves us well to recognize when we are ego-involved. We then have the opportunity step away and relate with a sense of ease and understanding.

Ego-involvement always hovers, ready to assert or protect how it believes things ought to be. Certainly, particular sensitivities and the degree of reactivity vary from person to person. Much of the time we do not even recognize we are ego-involved, such as "I must get this floor vacuumed." The "must" is a clue. As we become aware of ego-involvement we discover just how frequently we get hooked. We need to develop this awareness so that we can practice it as a meta-cognitive ability, The Rider in control.

Here is a list of a number of ways we can recognize that we have become ego-involved. *Use these moments to shift into the process of "becoming free."*

1. We notice ourselves reacting in any way.

2. We are attached to opinions, justifications, and judgments of many kinds, including right/wrong and good/bad in particular.

3. What we like and what we dislike (forms of judgment).

4. We also experience feelings ranging from dissatisfaction to intense desire.

5. Finally, some other key signs of ego-involvement are thinking in terms of "must," "should," "always," "never" as well as worrying and default mode negativity.

> *Use these moments to shift into
> the process of becoming free.*

ISSUES WITH EGO

With any reading of history, we will recognize how much Ego has driven the exercise of power and the terrible consequences both for subject people and often for the power-holders themselves. The military establishment of empires, the presumption of settlers of European origin in the "opening up of the West," thousands of years of despotic rule by the dynastic houses of China. All amazing histories wrought at a dreadful price in human suffering.

We replicate these patterns in our personal lives as individuals, couples, nuclear and extended families, and workplaces. Certainly, that is not always so. For instance, a person might be well liked and respected at work and be a martinet at home. Here I will take the general case and set aside the overlaps and complexities that arise.

Rather, I want to illustrate how ego-attachment generates distress and use a particular context as an example. Let me repeat a point that I made in the introductory chapter. Context only matters to the extent that we, as individuals, are ego-invested in it. Thus, politics matter to those whose identities are invested in politics. This idea applies just as much to someone who is self-critical (perfectionistic), as well as to any couple struggling in couplehood. Stresses at work, or in the family, being the "best mom" or "best dad," or in relating with your siblings, cousins, in-laws, and friends, — it does not matter. Context matters in that it reveals issues. A key part of what makes them issues in the first place are specific attachments. Let us take the context of being friends to illustrate what the attachments could be.

In doing this, insert any context you wish; I will personalize the example. "I feel swamped with all the media, Facebook, Twitter, Zoom and so forth. And there are my friends. I must keep in touch. I get no time to myself. I feel burdened and quite often feel resentful, and even get to feeling quite depressed. But I must keep up."

While core beliefs will be involved, exploring what I could be attached to can help me understand and work with "this stuff." Here are three examples of forms of attachment.

1. Attached to an evaluative identity: "I am spending so much time on my phone but am I being a good friend?" Self-doubt is fired up by self-critical (fault-finding) thinking. I try harder.

2. Attached to approval from other people: "Do they like me?" "What else do I need to do to show I am likeable?" Depending on the opinions of others, I am vulnerable. All too often we seek approval from those less likely to give it; their approval really counts! We tend to discount recognition easily given.

3. Attached to "being helpful," "fixing… .": "I have got to get back to her. She needs my help." It is possible she actually needs help. Leave that context aside. Rather, I am concerned about people who try to help even though conflict follows their efforts. Second, they believe they are doing it "for the other person," but they are "helping" to fulfil their own identity needs. Both motives may well be present. A fair test is how the "helper" reacts when the other person does not want to be helped.

We will explore attachment further particularly in Contrast #17 "Ego-attachment contrasted with *Natural Attachment*."

"WHAT IS" – BECOMING FREE

Because the ego is all about defining, it is easy to propose further definitions! Becoming free, on the other hand, is about an ongoing process, a way of being that flows and, in flowing, shifts. We can say we are becoming free as we release ourselves from the grip of ego. But what is this sense of inner freedom?

As we cultivate a sense of freedom, we will notice we stay in equanimity more easily. Reactivity is less frequent and increasingly easily released. We will have learned to stay out of distressing default modes of thought. Mental activity will generally be directed toward being present, appreciating "What Is," namely, the experience of the moment. We learn to engage playfully in situations, unattached to outcome and engage with life as possibility.

Somewhere in becoming free is acting to cultivate benefit. If we do not make this endeavor, we are restricting natural inclinations to connect and care. One way to cultivate benefit is to engage "playfully," where "play" is intended as something we do for its own sake (see Contrast #16). It is any activity we want to keep going because the activity is rewarding in and of itself. That is contrasted with doing something for what you can get out of it.

The core practices are to stop feeding the ego parasite (Practice #6.1) and engage in cultivating a sense of inner freedom (Practice #6.2). Since some readers may have some fear about this, we will consider that fear first.

The essence of such a fear would be if you believed that you are being asked to change yourself or to give up something that matters to you. This is simply not so. What is asked is that you first recognize ego-involvement. For example, "I don't like arguing," arguing in this context is the content. Ego- involvement operates in a self-sealing loop of Elephant poop.

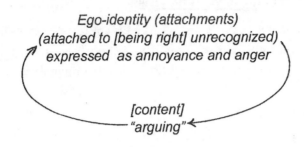

Ego-identity (attachments)
(attached to [being right] unrecognized)
expressed as annoyance and anger

[content]
"arguing"

Shift to splitting ego-involvement from whatever may be at issue. This takes us out of the loop into laying a path as we go along. Please note that what is "at issue" may be internal to you, such as worrying. Or, it may be interpersonal, and if it is interpersonal, there is most likely internal "stuff" going on at the same time. Both need attention. Laying a path as you go looks like this:

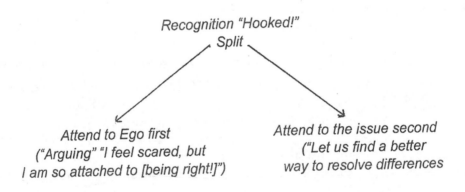

Recognition "Hooked!"
Split

Attend to Ego first
("Arguing" "I feel scared, but
I am so attached to [being right!]")

Attend to the issue second
("Let us find a better
way to resolve differences

We can attend to ego by using Practice 6.1 (below). Then, when you feel sufficiently at ease and you are operating as the Rider fully in control of how you engage, address whatever is at issue. Meanwhile, Practice #6.2 offers a starting point in becoming free. Subsequent Contrasts address specific aspects of attending to issues even as you cultivate peace of mind and a sense of inner freedom.

Practice #6.1
Catching Ego-Involvement

This practice involves taking Practice #2, Catching Content, deeper.

1. **Catch Ego-Involvement:** *Practice sensation awareness, sensations ranging from a clutch in the stomach to a "pressure" to argue, defend, prove, or perhaps over-ride the other person. Practice mental awareness, especially as demanding certainty, judgmental thinking, blaming, justifying, and worrying.*

2. **Name:** *"Hooked!" Breathe. When you have relaxed enough, go to the next point.*

3. **Take Time to Explore:** *Explore questions such as:*

    a. *"What am I trying to do?" You could start with the mental activities listed above. Find words that work for you.*

    b. *"How do I want (need) things to be?" and/or "What am I trying to get out of this?" Let answers just bubble up in your mind.*

    c. *"What does that tell me about my identity?" Or "What sort of person does that make me?" Or "What (or, who) am I trying to avoid being?*

4. **Letting go:** *"May I let go of this attachment." Try holding your arms downwards with hands open; relax your shoulders; imagine the ego-energy just draining out. Take relaxing breaths as you do this practice.*

Practice 6.2
Becoming Free

1. **Stabilize:** *Focus your awareness on the center of your forehead and hold that awareness. Breathe. Sense becoming centered.*

2. **Set your intention:** *What do you want to achieve that is likely to benefit both you and other people touched in the current situation?*

3. **Lay Down Your Path:** *"How can I act on my intention skillfully?" Intention acts as a compass setting a direction; seek an outcome without being attached to it. Act on what you can control. Negotiate what you cannot. Attend to what follows as it arises; stay away from trying to fix the future before it happens.*

CONTRAST #7

ADDICTED TO DRAMA contrasted
with *ALLOWING EQUANIMITY*

First, we will consider the idea of "being addicted" in a broad sense. Then a brief section on equanimity is offered by way of contrast. The subsequent section discusses our susceptibility to the dramatic and, finally, I have proposed that we have to be proactive if we choose to cultivate peace of mind and inner freedom.

"WHAT IS NOT" – ADDICTED

If you believe you are not addicted to drama, just watch your default thinking spring into action within seconds to settling down to relax, let alone meditate. Even when we go away on vacation, our brains may settle somewhat. We will notice the contrast and have the sense of enjoying ourselves. And we are enjoying ourselves. We allow a reduced level of stimulus. We believe that this is part of being on vacation. Yet, perhaps quite soon, we notice a sense of restlessness. What is there to do? How do we fill empty days? Perhaps we already have plans. Many people decide broadly months before a trip how they plan to spend the time.

All of that is the "What Is Not," the dramatic definitions out of which we spin our vacations and our everyday lives. No matter whether we dramatize through worry or by gossiping or in any other way, there is a biological component that we need to consider. Namely, our hormones and neural transmitters, once stimulated. They generate an on-going need for further stimulation. Our culture, with its emphasis on entertainment, schooling, and digital media contributes substantially to the initial stimulation and the on-going feeding of the system such that we want more much of the time. We can recognize this process at play and the role of the stories we tell ourselves and each other about needing or avoiding keeping in touch.

Where stimulation is concerned, we develop our own set-points in our need to feel stimulated. Under stimulated we feel bored; over-stimulated we feel stressed, even overwhelmed. At the same time, we tend to increase our tolerance for stimuli, especially in younger years. This has a survival benefit in that we generally cope well in emergencies. However, as we indulge our need for stimulus, we become addicted to the reward of feeling stimulated. For instance, worrying is initially more rewarding than the distress of feeling bored or simply allowing ourselves to be mentally still. We stimulate ourselves and contribute stimulation to each other by dramatizing our lives.

Correspondingly, we experience distress when we feel unstimulated. Given that we have habituated to high levels of stimulation, it is that much more challenging to release ourselves from the grip of drama.

"WHAT IS" – EQUANIMITY

When we seek to cultivate peace of mind and a sense of inner freedom, we come slap-bang up against that hunger for stimulation. It matters little whether we have to answer our cellphone or get bored waiting for an over-due plane to arrive. The circumstances are usually a secondary consideration. Rather, we ordinarily get distressed when our needs for stimulation are not met.

By way of contrast, we may cultivate equanimity. This goes against the grain for many, perhaps most of us. We must make a definite effort to experience equanimity. To make sense of the need to make this effort, let us consider the experience of equanimity.

The root of equanimity is in Latin "eaquus" – evenness, being equally held, and animus – spirit. If acceptance is being open to things being as they are, then equanimity is a particular way in which we hold our experience. That is, we hold it with an even spirit. Perhaps a brief example may help. For instance, suppose you feel stressed. There is a great difference between reacting, "Oh! I feel so stressed. I don't see how I can cope with all this stress. This is awful," and on you go raising your stress level even higher. Contrast that with responding, "Oh! I feel so stressed. Let me locate it in my body…. . Now breathe into it…. . Ah, relaxing. I see I am facing choices I am trying to avoid…."

As illustrated in that example, equanimity is not some state in which everything is peaceful and relaxed. Rather it is, as further examples will show, the capacity to be present to feeling bored without being distressed or attending to another person's anger and not taking it on such that we are personally at ease with the energy of anger. A tall order but equanimity can be cultivated.

"WHAT IS NOT" – DRAMA

To dramatize anything, we set up conflicting elements. It does not matter whether on the surface it is trivial, such as spilling some water, or something with major consequences, like having to declare bankruptcy. Something is wrong; something has to be done about it. Or perhaps it is inevitable; no matter, we do not accept it. We are into the story, the drama. I am suggesting we have a choice. We can continue to dramatize events, *or we can practice cultivating equanimity*. Understanding both brain and psychological functioning for each way of being can help inform our choice.

A major function of our brains is to make associations. Crucial to survival is coping with threats (tigers) and being alert to opportunities (food; sex, and in a modern context, experiencing an urgent need to answer the phone). The Elephant part of the brain reacts in a split second. The release of stress hormones is triggered, and our bodies can be in action before we have even thought about it. How many times might this fast brain reaction have saved your life on the highway?

Overall, we are stimulated; our Elephant is in action (review: The Elephant in Action, pp.11-13). Much of the day we are socially as well as mentally engaged in the drama of the moment. While patterns and levels of stimulation vary from person to person and situation to situation, we seek some level of intensity. If we observe ourselves, we will notice we are addicted to our preferred levels of stimulation. Shifting to "too much" or "too little," we experience physiological and emotional discomfort. Something will seem "off," discomforting or sometimes overwhelming.

At the same time, there are a number of immediate psychological gains derived from being engaged in drama. This is so even when the drama is "low key" such as having a friendly chat on the phone. These gains include:

1. A sense of mattering; personal meaningfulness, self-validation, for instance, asserting "my" opinion.

2. Energizing life; making day-to-day living interesting; feeling stimulated. Emotional states of this order are contrasted with feeling bored or neutral.

3. We get a sense of doing something by engaging in the drama irrespective of the content of the drama. For instance, by protesting world affairs to a group of friends, experientially it as if "I" am doing something for "the cause," no matter that I am not actually involved.

4. Bringing a sense of drama to the moment can be a way of connecting with other people, as in seeking sympathy or admiration or in affirming them.

5. Enacting our ego-identity. Each of us develops a unique personality such that we believe we have particular qualities. Being seen and seeing ourselves as having, or not having particular qualities is a major driver in our lives. For example, if I think of myself as generous, then I will have ways, my ways, of being generous. Or, if I do not like to see myself as selfish, and you suggest I am, just watch the reaction. *No matter what your ego-attachments may be, notice how you dramatize events. Then find the "ego-hook," "What am I attached to?"*

Notice how all those gains come about through processes of definition. This is why dramatizing is an aspect of "What Is Not." We bring these gains into being by acting dramatically. Instead pay attention to "dramatizing," the process, rather than the drama, the content (c.f.: Contrast #2). By recognizing dramatizing, we are in a position to opt for equanimity.

"WHAT IS" – ALLOWING EQUANIMITY

In dramatizing, we encounter a range of immediate experiences - excitement, distress, anger – the list goes on. Indeed, this is "what is," but which of these experiences do we want in the longer term? Indulging drama in present time undermines cultivating peace of mind and a sense of inner peace over time. The choice is clear. We can practice cultivating the immediate experience of equanimity, staying in a state of emotional evenness even in the face of stress or we can persist with drama. Trying to have both at the very least delays achieving peace of mind.

Cultivating equanimity is causally related to brain functioning. There are also psychological and social costs associated. Equanimity does not come free no matter that the longer-term gains are physical, emotional, and spiritual well-being.

Research reflecting the neurobiology of relaxation, let alone equanimity, is not as well established as it is for stress. Nonetheless two key aspects are clearly understood. The prefrontal cortex and the anterior cingulate cortex give us the capacity to act intentionally. Acting intentionally, we can exercise a measure of control over our physiology, emotions and thinking (Meaning-Making – Contrast #11).

Physiologically, we are capable of controlling our breathing, and we can relax intentionally. Likewise, we can choose to let our emotions flow through rather than acting out or repressing. Finally, with our thinking we can deliberately shift from one mode of thought to another. For example, we might choose to shift out of drama into grounding (Practice #.7.2 below). Making use of this neural capacity to change our mind is key to cultivating equanimity.

When we give up drama and cultivate equanimity, we are faced with two main psychological costs. One is giving up the stimulation of stress hormones. Stress hormones operate around a set point. Each of us learns to depend on a certain range of stimulation. Too much and we are overwhelmed; too little, we feel bored. When we practice cultivating equanimity, we are shifting our set point. We can experience some dis-ease, often as agitation, while we adjust.

The second cost is to our ego-identity. Ego is our Elephant trumpeting, needing to be seen and heard and whatever else our individual identities demand. This is a tough one to face. Nevertheless, when we are reactive or experience particular needs or the urge to dramatize, we can use those experiences as cues to explore core beliefs (Contrast #5).

The social costs of shifting from drama to equanimity can be considerable. People who know us are used to our patterns. They have developed their own ways of relating to our patterns as we have to theirs. Thus, when we are interacting, we engage at a relatively known level of drama enacted in fairly predictable ways.

Staying calm may not always be welcome, no matter what people have said. When we culti-vate equanimity, they are faced with a shift. There is a fair chance this shift will be questioned or even rejected, as in, "You're putting that on; I don't believe you." Or "You're not under-standing me. You don't care anymore." This second example can simply mean "you are not feeding my ego." Predictably, there will be some adjustment in your relationships depending upon how great a shift you are making, how you manifest that shift and how consistent you are. It is not unusual to find that you lose old friends and make new ones.

I have taken the position that dramatizing our lives gives us substantial gains, psychologi-cally and socially. But it costs us peace of mind. *Cultivating equanimity may entail some sense of loss and symptoms of withdrawal as we reduce our dependence on stress hormones. Practicing equanimity, however, is foundational to achieving peace of mind.*

**Practice #7.1
Cultivating Equanimity**

1. Notice, name the type of drama (4 possibilities below); accept the drama as "drama." No judgments; no explanations!

    a. "Spilt milk" – notice the reaction. Affirm "It happened."

    b. Reacting to another person(s) – take time; take space, as needed.

    c. Enmeshed in the past – core beliefs **

    d. Futurizing – rousing anxiety (counter with Practice #4 p.39)

2. Breathe, relax, take the observer role, and release the drama (see p.25 Processing).

3. Practice equanimity – go into the experience of the moment as deeply as you can – like diving into it and relaxing at the same time. Try to work with the question, "What is this ... (experience)?" not to come up with an answer. Rather to get deeper into the experience.

This practice is intended primarily to support working effectively with our emotional state. If we need to take remedial or preventive action, we can do so with equanimity and rationality.

** When we experience reactivity, needs, and urges to dramatize, we can use these experiences as cues that it is time to explore core beliefs (Contrast #5).

**Practice #7.2
Grounding**

This practice is intended to take you out of default thinking and into being present in your current environment.

Look around you. Name what you see – table, lamp, tree.

Continue for about a minute. Stop. If the default thinking starts up again, repeat the practice. Meanwhile it can be helpful to find a task to work on that requires your full attention.

In due course, attend to the needs underlying the default thinking in a beneficial way.

CONTRAST #8

"HAVING PROBLEMS" contrasted with *PLANNING*

Problems are generated when we define something as being wrong or being difficult about a situation. For example, criticizing, in the sense of finding fault, creates an event as a "problem." Other dimensions of "having problems" includes seeing defects in ourselves, relationship problems, issues at work and the conflicts that consume the world at large.

Planning determines a course of action to be followed usually aimed at achieving specified ends or may be a process plan, how we intend to go about doing something.

Pause for a moment. Shifting from having problems to *planning* can be a tall order. Most of us tend to be drama addicts, as was stressed in the previous Contrast. It can be like we are losing out by letting the drama go. "Who wants to do planning? It is so boring!" So, consider, are you ready to embrace equanimity and let the central drama of "I" go? If "Yes," then proceed. If not, then core beliefs are in control. I recommend you do more work with Contrast #4, Core Beliefs contrasted with *Exploration* (especially, p.47).

THE "WHAT IS NOT" OF "HAVING PROBLEMS"

When we examine "problems," we usually find a mindset that tends to notice what is wrong or, correspondingly, what could be different or better. Certainly, there are times that we need to deal directly with something being at issue. It is the role of *planning* to attend to resolving issues.

The mind set of "something wrong" generates internal and interpersonal distress. Notice how this is a process of definition that creates wrongness in the first place. We climb onto the Elephant of definition and feed it with stories, justifications and strongly held opinions. This is challenging enough for individuals, let alone in relationships in that we all have Elephants. They can start butting heads only too quickly.

Problems are so diverse content-wise that it can seem like something different is needed for each one. That diversity can become overwhelming. If, however, we shift from being caught up in the content to attending to the "What Is" of creating problems, then any problem is sufficient as an example. For instance: I say to my partner indignantly, "You promised we'd have time together tomorrow evening."

She reacts, "No, I never." And away we go into an argument about who is right and who is wrong. We have created a problem for ourselves, and we exacerbate the problem by indulging in an argument.

THE "WHAT IS" OF PLANNING

From a planning perspective with my partner's denial of what I had taken as a promise, I acknowledge something is amiss. That is, a situation that might be framed as a "problem" (what is wrong) is reframed as an "issue," that needs to be resolved. Planning is the Rider being in control of the Elephant. The Elephant may well not like it. Be prepared to train that elephantine part of your habitual thinking that, as examples, just wants to plunge into doing without following a plan or to avoid planning in the first place.

As guides to personal planning, each of the following questions is addressed below:

- *Seek to understand. What emotions need attention?*

- *What is at issue? Who owns the issue?*

- *What outcome or outcomes are we seeking to achieve? Attend to any differences.*

- *Allow that there can be mutually exclusive outcomes. This would be another issue to deal with that has a number of options.*

- *Given agreement over the desired outcome(s), create a plan – given "this situation," what do we want to achieve? Plan the desired outcome.*

- *Plan how we going to get there?*

Seeking to Understand – *Going into planning mode benefits from sensitivity. Sensitivity includes being sensitive to self, awareness of emotions, needs, beliefs, strengths, and limitations. And if another person or other people are involved in the planning process, inclusivity and mutual understanding are important. The planning process benefits when everyone feels included. We also need to understand each other's emotions and needs to the extent that we* can engage in planning with a fair measure of equanimity. At the same time, ensure that you do not get hooked into a story, that is, the problem.

It is crucial to validate each other's emotions as we seek to understand one another. We facilitate reaching mutual understanding when we express our emotions using "I" language, even in the privacy of our own thinking. No blame, no judgment, and we allow ourselves both to be heard and to hear ourselves. We need to be prepared for resistance. Sometimes we do not really want to hear or to share because we are acknowledging our vulnerability. It is like having a vulnerability mean that we are flawed in some way. This is a discomforting belief. We may block it off. Doing so can cost us a lot both personally and relationally.

Resistance to Planning – Part of the emotionality connected with resolving issues may be found in resistance to planning. Planning might seem to be a mechanical process. Maybe resistance stems from being attached to the drama of having a problem. We need to be willing to release ourselves from whatever is generating inertia if we are to allow internal peace to emerge.

Planning as Process – Determine what you want to achieve. If more than one person is involved, you do not need to have the same goals. If you have different goals, then how will you cooperate? What do each of you need to do to support the other to achieve your respective goals? If you have the same goals, then this is a collaborative process in which you combine your abilities and resources to achieve a shared goal.

In summary, no matter what is at issue, start by:

1. Being clear what is at issue – for one person or more?

2. For one person

   a. Is it a dilemma? What is needed to make a choice?

   b. Is it straight forward? Attend to blocks.

3. For more than one person

   a. Does this issue represent a difference between you? (Notice – no rights, no wrongs, no having to prove anything; no judgments; no justifications).

   b. Does the issue appear to belong to one person, such as, "I am worrying, and I recognize it is my stuff."

   c. Or is the issue about something that we own as a dyad (or family or another grouping)? Approach this issue as "ours," and plan collaboratively.

d. *Ensure that you stay with planning. It is a rational process. If emotions get aroused, then something else is stake, an emotional, ego-based problem is intruding. I recommend you get that problem resolved and then return to planning.*

Practice #8

Start by becoming aware of "having a problem" signed by thoughts such as "I have a problem," "Such-and-such is a problem," "This is crazy."

1. Breathe; relax.

2. Shift to planning (Rider takes control), as suggested above.

3. Attend to emotional well-being.

4. Make a plan, and follow through with the plan, or whatever else arises in following the course you choose.

5. **However, if** you are caught in the drama of the problem, review in terms of Contrast #6, Drama contrasted with Equanimity. **Or** are you resisting making the shift? If so, return to and practice Contrast #3, Resistance contrasted with Opening.

CONTRAST #9

TRUTH AND REALITY
"contrasted with *TRUTHS AND REALITIES*

This section contrasts what we believe things to be with how we generate our immediate experience moment by moment. **Ordinarily we act as if Truth exists independently of our own being and as if there is a single Reality in which we all participate.**

IN DOING SO,
WE SEPARATE OURSELVES FROM THAT WHICH WE OBSERVE.
THIS SEPARATION IS "WHAT IS NOT."

This perspective, no matter how true it appears, depends upon a combination of belief and definition. It is a perspective that brings detached observation into being – "I" am the observer of a separate "it." It is crucial to recognize **the role of observation** in this contrast. We will take this further after introducing the contrasting perspective.

This Contrast is grounded in the recognition that nothing can be known independently of the knower. This perspective permits recognition of the connection between the knower and the known. This connection is "What is," and this constitutes our immediate experience. **However, we think and act as if what we know exists independently of us.** This separation is "What is not." At times, this perspective is useful. Much of the time it gets us into a lot of trouble.

Connection is generated by the knower applying her or his way of knowing to the object experienced. Thus, within the constraints of culture and socialization, each of us carries our own truths and generates our own realities. Our truths and our realities constitute "what is," we then act in relation to our constructions. In this conception of existence, "truth" and "reality" are indicated by the use of lower-case "t" and "r" respectively. Whereas the upper-case, bolded letters **T** and **R** refer respectively to **T**ruth as absolute and to **R**eality as being a single reality with universal access.

If we take this contrast seriously, the implications for how we live and for the quality of our lives are wide-ranging and substantial. We will address the major implications in this section. For simplicity, I will call the detached perspective "**Realism**" and *the connected perspective "Meaning-Making."*

THE "WHAT IS NOT" OF REALISM

We are socialized into the dominant cultural belief that there is a **R**eal **W**orld out there. This **R**eal **W**orld is knowable. Likewise, absolute **T**ruth exists, and it is discoverable. Well, this is so, isn't it? After all, when "I" look at a table, it is a real table that I am looking at. And when "I" got rear-ended last week, I got rear-ended. "It's silly to say that reality doesn't exist, that it is all belief. Kind of nutty – right!"

You certainly observe and experience the world around you. You are aware of a myriad of interactions with other people and a wide range of other events as separate events. Even TV seems real, and it is certainly separate from you.

So why is it "What Is Not"? The fundamental error is separating ourselves conceptually from our environment and then acting in relation to our conception, generating separateness and not our immediate experience, our immediate connection. Note, this includes our internal environment. For instance, I can refer to "my eyes" or "my stomach." I take them as parts of me, like a carburetor or a rubber tire. This is the beginning of separation. We add layers of meaning, perhaps "My eyes are too small," or "My stomach is too big." We elaborate these beliefs and meanings to define our personalities, our values, lifestyles, other people, our communities, nations, forests, oceans... on and on.

Our sense of separation is exacerbated through our dependence on language. Language functions by making distinctions, and the easiest ones to work with are those that make clear separations, namely all the language we use in defining. We see the beginning of this process in distinguishing tables from chairs and dogs from cats.

The crucial benefit derived from separateness is survival. Beyond survival, by acting on the world and modifying it, we create the means to flourish. Without separateness, starting as children, we would fall downstairs or get run over by cars. Our cities, our technologies, our health care, abundant food supplies and so forth all depend on how we separate innumerable entities and then use those separations for good or ill.

The major downside is that we do the same thing to ourselves, our relationships and to how we experience life. We turn processes into objects. As objects, they can be manipulated. I outlined the upside in the previous paragraph, but the costs of separation are enormous: wars, famine, greed, murder, drugs, family violence, anger in the workplace, hate between groups and self-directed anger.

THE "WHAT IS" OF MEANING-MAKING

We ascribe meaning to every event that enters our conscious awareness and to many that are held preconsciously. **"Events" refer to anything and everything we attend to.** *It is also important to understand "meaning" as I use the word:* **"meaning" is whatever we say or think (including bodily reactions) about an event, any event.** *In large measure "meaning" is how we define events, for example, seeing the traffic light is red, means "stop."*

It is not that we are making meaning that matters here. That goes on mostly below the level of conscious awareness. The "What Is" is actually recognizing that we are attributing meaning to events, preferably but not necessarily in the moment of doing so (Practice #2.2, p.29, attends to this recommendation). We are then in the driver's position of being able to choose what we do with the meanings we are generating.

Overall generating separateness dominates our lives. It is habitual, fast, and often useful, if not necessary. *However, we can derive three major benefits by attending to the "What Is" of Meaning-Making. We become increasingly aware of being in control of how we encounter our lives experientially. We can enhance our sense of aliveness by living in the moment, and we can deepen our sense of connection with other people and the world in general. If we take this practice on, we also need to accept some "downsides." First, it takes mental effort to work with meanings as we generate them (Contrast #4). While it is preferable to catch meaning-making in the moment, it is worth attending to in hindsight. In this way, we can develop our capacity to work with Meaning-Making with increasing rapidity, ease, and skill. Second, we also need to be willing to relinquish a whole lot of drama (Contrast #7). Finally, we need to learn* when to stick with **Realism** *and when to work with Meaning-Making.*

- *As a rule of thumb, the* **Realist** *perspective works well for practical tasks, emergency situations and casual, non-contentious interactions.*

- *For most of the rest of our lives, if we want peace of mind and a sense of freedom, then we want to adopt the Meaning-Making perspective.*

The next Contrast, #10, addresses when to stay with **Realism** and when to attend to Meaning-Making.

APPRECIATION AS AN ANTIDOTE TO REALISM

*Take **appreciation** as the experience of **taking in and cherishing** the moment, as one might in smelling a sweetly-scented flower. Taking in the scent, the preciousness of the sweetness, is an experience of appreciation. In that moment, there is no separate "you" nor is there a separate flower. There is a connectedness, awareness of immersion in scent-experience; This is the sense of connectedness that I am calling "appreciation."*

***Practicing Appreciation** – The practice is to fully imbibe the experience. For a moment at least there is no "I," no "other." Yet, at the same time, we value the experience. In principle, this applies to every experience, even the most distressing ones. That is a tall order, but we can head in that direction.*

The results can be quite surprising. We can learn to treasure even challenging times but start at the easy end. Identify what you already appreciate in the way described here. Then learn to extend the range of events that you appreciate. Do this intentionally on a daily basis. Also, practice cultivating appreciation through senses you do not ordinarily use in this way. Contrast #19 details this approach.

SUMMARY

The ideas that have been presented in this contrast are quite complex. I have summarized the Contrast in the following table:

Realism	*Meaning-Making*
Reality: There is a single, ultimate **Reality**. All of us have at least partial access to **Reality**.	***realities:** Whatever we experience as "real" is constructed as relations between the observer and the observed. This is a complex interaction between social, psychological, and ultimately unknowable external phenomena.*
Truth: There is a single, final, knowable universal truth, **The Truth**. Individually and collectively, we search for the **Truth**. The certainty of the **Truth** is, in principle, testable.	***truths:** Individually and collectively, we generate our own truths. Each truth is valid within its own frame of reference. This means all truths are equally valid (but are rarely equally valued!).*

Right/Wrong; True/False: Knowing or claiming to know "The Truth" sets up the dichotomies of right/wrong, true/false and from there, we quickly get to good/bad, better/worse and judgments of all kinds.	*same/different: With all truths being valid, we will either hold the same truths or our truths will be different. The question now becomes "What do we do with this difference?" (We can take a "difference" as an opportunity to negotiate.)*
Justification Using Causal Explanations: Belief in Truth, Reality and Causality allows us to generate "causal explanations" as justifications. Such explanations make the claim: "'This' causes 'that.'" Causal explanations answer the question "Why?" Causal explanations work well for mechanics; applying them to living beings, we mislead ourselves and other people.	*explanation in Meaning-Making is concerned with describing how things work, that is, process descriptions. "When I put these seeds in soil, keep them moderately warm and give them water, they will sprout in a few days." This addresses the question, "How?"*
Language of Defining: By defining we create a world and all aspects of it as being Real, solid, and separate. We define primarily by using: **Labels:** names, categories, types **Judgments:** could/should, shouldn't, good/bad, right/wrong, better/worse etc., (including making comparisons) **Criticisms:** blaming, accusing and similar types of statement, self-criticism	*language of description: When we describe we identify how different elements are connected. We describe primarily by referring to:* *sensing: seeing, touching, body sensation, emotion, and hearing.* *meta-cognitive awareness: "looking in from above" to describe our cognitive and sensory processes, including thoughts, feelings and sensations, motivations, intentions, and expectations.*
Explaining: takes many forms including excusing **Justifying:** a form of explaining **Worrying** **Stories** and **Opinions** **Realist language** emphasizes **nouns** and **adjectives.** Nouns and adjectives generate separation.	*planning: describing how we intend to achieve a stated goal or undertake a specified process.* *"Meaning-Making language": specifically in describing, verbs show the connection between the elements described.*

The Individual is "objectified," being understood as composed of different qualities. Within the **Realist** frame-of-reference, we tend to view each other as both determined (cannot help being what we are) and as possessing free will (willful), such that we may on occasion be held responsible for other people's choices as well as blaming others for our own choices.	*"The individual" is understood as "having agency," that is, we possess a natural capacity to make choices. Indeed, we lay down our life paths as an ongoing process of choosing. Investing ourselves in the Meaning-Making perspective implies that, increasingly, we become aware of our moment-by-moment choosing and take responsibility for our choices.*
Commentary: The Realist mind-set dominates in human society. Realism is appealing in that it provides a sense of certainty, simplicity (if/then logic), efficiency (only one person is required to make decisions) and frequently immediate gratification through the exercise of power. Benefits tend to be short-term.	*commentary: The Meaning-Making perspective is present in our thinking, but it gets buried easily by **Realist** definition. Adopting a Meaning-Making perspective in relating entails two or more people seeking to understand each other and working out mutually acceptable arrangements. This takes time, energy, and a lot of thought.* *Benefits tend to be long-term.*

Practice #9
Practicing Appreciation

1. Get in touch with the act of appreciating – Identify situations in which you already experience appreciation; moments you cherish. Practice them a number of times (5 – 10) each day (examples: mealtimes, showering, being with plants and trees). Take in the awareness of doing this. Recognize you can do so intentionally.

2. Identify situations that you might appreciate if you were to engage that way. Practice at least 6 times every day.

3. Notice getting hooked into the **Reality** of your thoughts – pause, breathe, releasing all judgments, pull in the experience. Feel it. Imbibe it – treasure that you are alive to the moment – Wow! Make a point of doing this three times a day until appreciation is established as a habit.

CONTRAST #10

STAYING WITH "WHAT IS NOT"
contrasted with
STAYING WITH "WHAT IS"

WHEN TO STAY WITH "WHAT IS NOT"

In the previous contrast, I suggested that, as a rule of thumb, stay with "What Is Not" for practical tasks, emergency situations and in casual, non-contentious interactions. There are two specific sets of circumstances in which shifting to "What Is" is worthy of consideration. One is when you find yourself holding opinions as The Truth, as if they exist independent of your meaning-making, or when you are really stuck on your opinions. The second is in the arena of conflict between yourself and a partner, relative or friend, and possibly in work situations.

HOLDING "THE TRUTH" AND STRONG OPINIONS

When you find yourself holding "The Truth," that something is true in some absolute sense, its truth has nothing to do with you. Obvious examples include: God exists versus no God, and Good and Evil exist as competing, cosmological forces versus people in the world being judged as good or evil. When you notice you hold a belief in this way, as inherent truth, flag it.

Closely related are strong opinions and identifications. They have a comparable effect on our thinking and bear upon our actions. It is difficult to give examples that would apply to everyone. Rather there are classes of opinions that can help you recognize when you are caught up in something being "The Truth." Explanations are a major class. Even to maintain that the diversity of life on Earth is explained by evolution is a case in point, or conversely to hold to the idea that we are result of Intelligent Design.

Justifications represent another major class of opinions. Any time we justify anything, we are appealing to definition and belief. Holding that a justification is warranted may be so, but we can delude ourselves too. For instance, "being late for work because… " is necessarily expressed from within a frame-of-reference. The example begs the question of starting out for work earlier, for instance. All too often what we might think of as a valid justification is heard by the other person as an excuse, that we are failing to take responsibility for our actions.

Our primary concern here is for cultivating peace of mind and a sense of inner freedom. We are not concerned about whether something is true, or justifications are warranted. *Rather, we are concerned about what we are doing with that truth and how we relate to it effects our well-being.*

There is a range of consequences for believing in The Truth and in maintaining strong opinions as unquestionable. Religious wars and the consequences of racism are major examples. If you are willing to question belief, then you are likely to find value in shifting to the "What Is" of becoming free no matter what the belief may be.

On the other hand, if you are willing to take full responsibility for holding such a belief, you may choose to live that belief. Does that give you, or anyone else for that matter, the right to impose such beliefs on another person? Although I used examples with consequences for millions of people, the same dynamics plays out for couples, families, in the workplace and so forth. Where stresses exist, examining the impact of our deeply-held beliefs can lead us to interact with other people in new ways, ones that are conducive to everyone's well-being.

CONFLICT

Conflict between people arises from all kinds of differences. All of them are grounded one way or another in opinions and beliefs. The nature of conflict ranges. At one extreme is what may be taken as a "small moment," a side-ways look from a friend. At the other extreme is war. In between, so many varieties of conflict arise, such as in difficult intimate relationships, competitive work situations and the aftermath of car accidents.

Despite appearances, conflict is rarely trivial. **Trivial** means that a point is objectively verifiable independently of anyone's opinion. For example, there is one correct total when we add up a column of numbers. Any other total is in error. For all other conflicts there are deeper issues at stake, including ego-attachment (see: directly relevant Contrasts #6, #13, and #17). In that such issues are rarely addressed, conflicts especially in ongoing relationships tend to reoccur one way or another. Shifting to "What Is" is one way of attending to the deeper issues and releasing distress.

Our habitual ways of thinking tend to bind us into the realm of "What Is Not" when conflict arises. Other options exist.

Attending to Differences – When conflict arises, often it can be resolved relatively easily. Start by validating each other's positions. Validation means being clear what the other person's position is and accepting it. The conflict often has little to do with Truth. Rather, identify where you differ, and negotiate a win-win solution to the difference.

Hostile Conflict – Hostile conflict may be said to exist when one or more parties to a conflict insists on a position and will not consider differences. Taking a position in this way asserts "The Truth," in effect, "I am right. You are wrong, and that is that." For the most part, positions come in the form of justifications, opinions, beliefs, memories, fears, and expectations. Thus, in taking a position the person has invested themselves in "What Is Not." Now you have the option of staying with "What Is Not" or shifting to "What Is."

If you choose to stay within the frame-of-reference undergirding your opinion, then turn to the principle you are upholding (e.g. Fairness). Be sure you are prepared to stand by it. Be aware that arguing particulars, such as who said what when, leads to entanglements. *If you choose not to assert the principle, go to "What Is" and assert boundaries rather than engage in a stress-inducing back-and-forth.* Otherwise, you are accepting the burden of proof. If the other person has the power to accept or reject your evidence, be circumspect about what you choose.

Communicating – How we communicate with one another on a turn-by-turn basis has major implications for how the interaction unfolds. Any reactivity needs to be resolved before endeavoring to discuss an issue and negotiate differences. The next Contrast, #11, examines communicating in some detail.

Stories play important roles in our lives, no matter that they represent "What Is Not." It is worth considering what roles they might play. Secondly, what we define the stories to be, let alone what the stories themselves define, bears reflection. On the other hand, how we tell our stories effects both how they are likely to be heard and how we constrain or liberate ourselves in our story-telling. For these reasons, stories and story-telling are considered in Contrast #12.

WHEN TO STAY WITH "WHAT IS"

Certainly, there are many situations in which being present to the "What Is" of our experience is generally beneficial. Moments of intimacy and enjoying meals together are instances. What

I am concerned with in this Contrast are those occasions in which we all too easily get caught up in "What Is Not" and may truly benefit by staying with "What Is." Those occasions are when conflict is in the offing.

We should benefit by attending to "What Is" in four sets of circumstances associated with conflict. This includes releasing ourselves both from ego-attachment and attachment to particular outcomes (Contrasts #17 and #18 respectively).

FOUR CIRCUMSTANCES FOR STAYING WITH "WHAT IS"

Emotions are aroused
Conflict is erupting
Strong opinions are expressed
Being caught up in default thinking

While there is overlap between these situations, think of them as forming a Venn diagram that shows how much different elements overlap. The area in common for all four of these circumstances is being ego-involved in content around which conflict swirls. Making the shift from being ego-involved to taking control through meta-cognitive awareness is conducive to cultivating benefit, as well as over time achieving peace of mind and a sense of freedom. Attending to ego-involvement is key and has been addressed especially in Contrast #6.

Emotions Are Aroused – This refers to emotions arising from ego-identity. These emotions, or feelings, are mostly aversive. The most obvious ones are anger, anxiety, embarrassment, defensiveness, guilt, fears (but not all fear), hurt, jealousy, resentment, self-righteousness, and shame. There are also feelings of "desire," including feeling driven, self-centered ambition, gloating, greed, lust (possessiveness) and being superior.

Noticing any of those feelings represent opportunities for practicing self-awareness and exploration of the ego-attachments they represent. Work with Practice #10 as well as Practices #6.1 and 6.2. Keep in mind that these are practices and thus done over and over again.

Conflict is Erupting – As conflict arises, the "What Is" includes the body tensing, intensifying emotions and defensive/reactive thoughts. A key skill here is to be alert to tension arising. The sensation of tension is often felt in the stomach, but there can be other cues such as increasing heart-rate, frowning or your cheeks heating up. Taking care of our bodily sensations is a capacity that is worth developing.

All too often tension has been present or rising for a while before we notice it. Learning to tune in at the outset and attending to feelings and attachments early can prevent a lot of conflict. Either way, take space from the conflict and get your emotions settled. Once settled, it is much easier for you, as the Rider, to guide the Elephant and direct how you interact with the other person.

Strong Opinions – *In the face of strong opinions, which include those grounded in legality, morality, or politics, you are choosing not to oppose by shifting to "What Is." Two viable alternatives are:*

1. ***Getting curious*** - *What can you learn from the other person so as to understand how they come to hold their position so strongly, or what else might you learn constructively from the situation?*

2. ***Take care*** *of your own feelings and meanings. It is quite possible to feel awkward or take on being weak by choosing not to oppose. No matter what these feelings and meanings are, they need to be honored (see: Contrast #17, especially pp.121--122) and then released. Cultivating peace of mind implies that if you choose not to confront, then accept making that choice. Release any inclinations either to justify your choice or to beat yourself up mentally for so choosing.*

Being Caught Up in Default Thinking – *First, we need to be aware of the patterns that serve as our default modes of thought (Contrast #4). Common ones include blaming, criticizing, climbing into fears, futurizing (inducing anxiety) and other forms of worrying. "What Is" is practiced by recognizing that we have climbed into a default mode and make the mental effort to step out of it (Practice #4, p.39).*

Being able to discriminate and choose when to stay with "What Is Not" and when to switch to "What Is" is a significant skill. This provides distinct ways of engaging with particular circumstances. Either choice made appropriately is conducive to cultivating peace of mind and inner freedom.

Practice #10
Opening to Emotions

1. Stay prepared to recognize ego-attached emotions arising, especially when you are entering situations in which they are likely to arise. Use a flash card, for example: "Feeling?" One word can remind you to shift from being driven by ego (Elephant) into the awareness of being caught-up (Driver taking control of the mental Elephant).

2. Breathe, sense the feeling (locate associated sensations in your body if you can. You may or may not be able to locate physical sensations, especially when this practice is new to you).

3. Take time to explore – Use the questions listed under "Exploration" p.47 selectively. Allow the practice to develop. This is not intended to be difficult, rather it is a matter of arousing curiosity.

CONTRAST #11

ORDINARY COMMUNICATION
contrasted with *MEANING-MAKING*

"WHAT IS NOT" – ORDINARY COMMUNICATION

The "What Is Not" of ordinary, day-to-day communication is that we define what the other person says and shows non-verbally as having particular meanings. We do so in a matter of milliseconds. We then act or react to our definitions as if those meanings were contained within the message. It is as if these solid messages are shuttled back-and-forth, weaving the cloth of interactions. This is a "mechanical" way of communicating and understanding how we communicate. I will give an example of Mechanical Communication as a vehicle for describing how this mind set works.

The "What Is Not" of ordinary communication is brought into being as each person defines the other person's communication and acts in relation to that definition. First, it is important to recognize that for most interactions communicating mechanically is normal, habitual, and efficient. It breaks down in the face of disagreement. *As soon as any disagreement appears, shift to the Meaning-Making perspective, and attend to the "What Is" of our experience of the communication.*

Example: What happened for Sarah and Steven the other morning happens for us over and over and in so many different ways. Sarah had gone shopping. Arriving home, she opened the backdoor and called, "Hello! I'm home!"

Steven, from the basement, yelled, "I'm washing!" His tone sounded sharp. Sarah felt her tummy tighten. Steven came upstairs and demanded, "Why do you always yell at me like that when you come in?"

Sarah could see it coming. It didn't matter what she did, Steven would be mad at her. She felt angry and reacted sharply, "I don't always yell at you. I was just letting you know I am home." She adds indignantly, "Aren't you glad I'm back and I have done the shopping."

Steven was really mad now. "You come in. You immediately want to know where I am. There's no space for me. And I don't care a goddamn that you've done all the shopping!"

You can guess where this fight is going.

Let us unpack this incident using the Mechanical Model (illustrated on the next page):

Sarah arrives home. She believes she is sending Steven a "gift," namely, letting him know she is home. She intends to let him know she is glad to be back with him and to reassure him that it is she and not an intruder that has come in.

Steven has already defined the message as intrusive, and he takes it that Sarah is too dependent on him. He reacts by accusing Sarah of yelling at him. His response is depicted as a bomb in the diagram. It explodes in Sarah's world, and she reacts defensively. This process of definition and reaction continues. The fight is on.

In the diagram, the "Mechanical Model" shows communication and the environment as solid lines as if they exist independently of us. Sarah and Steven are shown as a series of dashes to indicate their "permeability" to solid messages being shuttled between them.

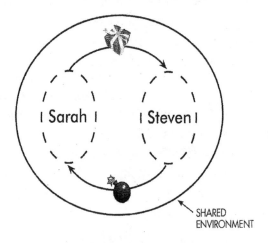

SHARED
ENVIRONMENT

Communicating – The Mechanical Model

This type of communication has a profound impact on any relationship when there is disagreement. More generally, our habitual use of communicating mechanically has a bearing on how we connect with other people, and it affects the quality of our intimate relationships in profound ways.

"WHAT IS" – MEANING-MAKING

The "What Is" of communicating from within the perspective of "Meaning-Making" is imme-diate and experiential. **The key point is that either as speaker or listener, we attend to our own meanings regarding what is said and done.** This integrates feelings, emotions, beliefs and sensations with thought and speech. Combined, they represent the experiential truth for each person. This perspective also holds that each person is fully and totally responsible for what they say and what they do.

> The "What Is" of Meaning-Making is the personal truth of our immediate experience. When we share our experience, we can be said to "be in truth." How we then conduct ourselves is sub-stantially our own choice.

I will illustrate how this model works with a replay of the story of Sarah and Steven during which they shift into the "Gardening Model." In this model, each communication ("xxx" and "yyy") are but sounds. The speaker loads the words and gestures with meaning, the recipi-ent attributes their own meaning. If there is an acceptable match between their respective meanings, all is well. But if they mismatch, conflict arises unless they have cultivated the communication skills to cope with mismatches beforehand.

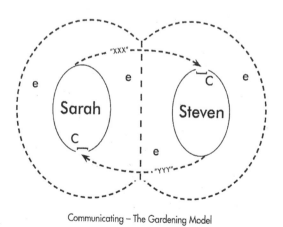

Communicating – The Gardening Model

Sarah and Steven have been learning to stay with "What Is" in communicating. They are working with "The Gardening Model." It is not easy for them to change habits of a lifetime, but then cultivating any garden is demanding work. Cultivating a relational garden is that much more demanding.

The story starts at the same point. Sarah had gone shopping. Arriving home, she opened the backdoor and called, "Hello! I'm home!"

Steven, from the basement, yelled, "I'm washing!" His tone sounded sharp. Sarah felt her tummy tighten.

Steven came upstairs and demanded, "Why do you always yell at me like that when you come in?"

Sarah, moving towards a chair, asked, "Can we sit down and see where each of is coming from?"

Steven heaved a sigh and responded gruffly, "Yeah," paused and asked sharply "Well?"

Sarah felt her tummy tighten still more. "I'm feeling all tensed up. How are you feeling?"

Steven, said guardedly, "I'm okay." He thought about "I." "No, I'm not. I'm tense, too."

Moments of truth; now there is hope.

Sarah asked, "Can we see what was going on for each of us?"

Steven: "Yes. It's like you can't leave me alone. You have to know where I am, and I've got to be here for you all the time. You're so co-dependent!"

Sarah: "It's like I can't leave you alone."

Steven: "That's right."

Sarah is getting how powerful that is for Steven and responds, "That is so powerful for you, and absolutely not what I want!" She sees Steven's face soften some. "Would you be willing to hear where I was coming from?"

Steven: "Okay."

Sarah: "Certainly I want to let you know I'm home. I am glad to be back with you, and I want you to know that it is me and not someone breaking in."

Steven: "Oh, really?"

Sarah: "Yes, really!"

Steven, relaxing, taking in the implications: "I'm feeling so soft. Wow. So different... almost unbelievable. Yes, different meanings and this could have gone so off-track. So, let's figure out what each of us needs now... ."

Notice how easily that interaction could have gone off track. However, both rather tentatively stayed present to their respective truths, heard each other without blame or judgment, and both felt validated.

More on the Gardening Model, it represents communication and the environment with broken lines. This is intended to indicate that meanings are personal; those held by one person may well be different than those held by another. The solid line representing each person signals that what we hear, see, and do gets constructed from within the individual's mental-emotional frame of reference for making meaning. The "C" in the diagram indicates that we are making the connection between what we perceive and our particular way of making meaning.

Let us unpack the Sarah and Steven scenario in terms of the Gardening Model. Both versions start the same way. They diverge when Sarah attends to her feelings and cultivating openness, instead of reacting mechanically.

Acknowledging their feelings allows them both to begin to listen to each other. Sarah gets the powerful meaning Steven attributes to her "calling out" to him. Her validating him opens the gateway to further understanding.

Once each person understands the other, there is space to attend to the difference. Key to this phase is to articulate the difference, validate it and address each person's underlying need.

Because it is expressed as definition, Mechanical Communication represents an exercise in power (see: Contrast 15). The effect is to direct, restrict or close off opportunities. There is one major exception, and that is "We/They" language. *Connection is strengthened for whoever constitutes "we" when we speak in terms of the inclusive "we."* The exercise of power is the separation created in defining "them" as "them," irrespective of who or what constitutes "them."

I am not claiming that Mechanical Communication is wrong, bad, or harmful, and certainly this is not so in and of itself. Rather, each form of communication has its place. *Gardening communication opens opportunities, and hence may be understood as the expression of love (see: Contrast #15). Herein lies some of the "vulnerability" of this approach to communicating. Participants need to be open to understanding each other for this approach to be helpful.*

Mechanical Communication is unilateral, defining exercises power one-way, or two-ways if there is competition over whose definition counts. Recipients of such communications are left with a limited number of options. These are principally to agree or comply, to avoid or contest.

On the other hand, gardening communication is two-way. It can only truly function if both (or all) participants collaborate. This can happen naturally during courtship, for instance, but too soon that flow is interrupted by definition.

Gardening Communication is not a panacea; it can be misused. For instance, one person can sound like "being understanding" matters to them, but underneath that person has a power agenda. That agenda gets exposed sooner or later when it becomes apparent that one person is not really interested in understanding the other and issues are not getting resolved.

Another possibility is that no matter how well-intentioned two people may be, we can come up against irreconcilable differences. Perhaps it is less harmful to honor those differences and say "Goodbye" than land up fighting.

Applying the Gardening Model, especially in close relationships, supports the development of mutuality, cordiality, and a deeper appreciation for one another. Taking each other into account requires conscious and on-going effort. Whereas defining takes extraordinarily little effort, and we gain efficiency, but efficient often comes with a cost in close relationships.

These models of communication differ on several dimensions. They are compared in the summary that follows.

SUMMARY

"What Is Not" The Mechanical Model of Communication	*"What Is"* *The Gardening Model* *of Communication*
Communication is enacted and understood in terms of definition.	*Communication is understood as meaning-making by each individual from within learned and variably shared frames of reference.*
Meaning resides in the message.	*Meaning is constructed by individuals from within their own frame of reference.*
Listeners ordinarily assume that meanings they attribute are what was intended by the speaker.	*Listeners appreciate they are generating meanings and are alert to the possibility of discrepancies in the meanings arising between them.*

Speakers and listeners assume they are talking about the same reality. Hence, any misunderstanding implies someone is at fault.	*Speakers and Listeners assume they occupy different realities. Differences in meaning serve as opportunities to learn about each other and to negotiate those differences.*
Communication tends to be competitive and tends to generate win/lose situations. Polite communications sustain equilibrium.	*Communication tends to be collaborative and invites negotiation. There is the possibility for deep connection and understanding between people.*
This model is robust to the extent that people accept or tolerate the definitions put forth, but when we try to impose our definitions (meanings and opinions) conflict in one form or another ensues.	*This model is fragile in the sense that to function it depends upon the willingness of both (all) participants to collaborate.*

Practice #11.1
Releasing Agenda

Noticing when you are approaching someone with an agenda (for instance wanting them to change or behave differently). Practice one of these three options:

1. Identify and release the agenda; release your own ego-attachments.

2. Meta-communicate: negotiate the agenda. If the other person is receptive at least to considering your agenda, proceed. If not, go to the next option, #3.

3. Attend to the "drive" you experience to assert your agenda: what is your need that you want the other person to fulfill? How can you attend to your own need?

Practice #11.2
Shift from "React" to "Response"

1. Be alert to reacting. This happens so quickly, but sometimes we can anticipate when it may happen. Then be alert and remain calm. Notice yourself reacting; create a pause and breathe.

2. Identify what you are feeling – 3 or 4 words "I am feeling ... ." and/or share what you are inclined to do reactively (e.g.: argue!) without doing it. Also: no justification, blame nor judgment.

3. Cultivate responding, "How can I handle this constructively?" If ideas do not come immediately, take time, and set boundaries as needed to find a way to act beneficially.

CONTRAST #12

STORIES:
WHAT WE TELL contrasted with *HOW WE TELL THEM*

Story is intended in the broadest sense. **A story** is anything we say **about** an event (phenomenon) that gives it meaning. To say that the sun rises at 6:30 in the morning identifies an event, not a story. To add, "I like to get up to watch it" is the beginning of a story. That "'I' want to get up to watch it" is being said about the sunrise, and "me," and that could be fleshed out from there.

A story in and of itself performs the role of defining and constitutes "What Is Not." Our immediate experience, "What Is," gets embedded in the stories we tell. In saying more about any story, we pile on layers of meaning and belief. We then act in relation to the story, caught up in the power of "What Is Not."

In no way do I intend to condemn stories, far from it. Rather I intend to alert us to the power of stories and of storytelling. Stories represent a crucial component of human history. They bring along with them all the tragedy and all the amazingness that constitutes our lives. We can move towards enlightenment by learning from stories. Life can also be a living hell by virtue of the stories within which we are enmeshed.

The power of stories is the power to define the quality of our lives. For example, if our story is centered on growing up in an alcoholic family, we may live out the rest of our lives according to whatever it means to us to be a child of an alcoholic parent. That is just one example. The point is that each of us necessarily grows up with a life history, a multifaceted and multilayered story. This is the legacy we receive, like it or not. What we can do with that legacy is an entirely different matter. Indeed, one set of options is offered in this book.

We live our lives from within our stories, telling them in habitual ways. To the extent we experience distress in our lives, it is the **way** in which we tell the story integrated with the meanings we attribute to the story that generate distress. **It is not the content.**

We can also learn to unmask distress-inducing beliefs as well as the ego-gratification embedded in the way in which we tell our stories. We can also learn how to tell our stories with compassion, including self-compassion. This shift supports achieving peace of mind and release from self-imposed burdens.

ASPECTS OF "WHAT IS NOT" IN STORY-TELLING

Let us start with two premises:

1. We always tell a story for a reason. We may or may not be conscious of our reasons.

2. Ordinarily we have deeper motivations; some are held preconsciously and others we can identify.

There is value in recognizing both reasons and underlying motivations. That level of awareness allows us to engage reflectively and *attend to the "What Is" level of story-telling.*

Reasons for telling stories include:

1. **Justifying** – We may have a strong drive to justify all kinds of actions ranging from "Why I didn't call" to "Why going to war is warranted." Justification takes many forms, including justifying judgments and values. With self-observation, we notice that a lot of our self-talk is intended to justify whatever it is we want to justify, such as anger, resentment, pride and so on.

2. **Influence** – We seek to influence other people in many ways. The examples that follow are not mutually exclusive: entertain (amuse), court, impress, persuade, prejudice, divert attention, scare or seduce.

3. **Identity and Tradition** – We can tell stories to secure or expand both our identity (who we are as individuals, groups etc.) and our traditions. Ordinarily, the two will be interrelated. Many stories associated with identity are focused on that of an individual, but certainly this is not necessarily so. For example, stories of heroism in a family might be told as part of the family history and, hence, identity. Such a family might celebrate June 6, (D-day, 1944) each year as a mark of respect, affirming the roles of family members in various wars.

4. **Belief** – Many stories are told as an expression of belief and as explanations of phenomena or of mysteries. Such stories range from those told by the great religions of the world to why Aunt Mary is so strange.

Motives for telling stories take us into the mystery of being human. Why we think we are telling a story and what actually motivates us can be different. Reflecting on this point could serve us well. *Identifying our motives can help us attend to the "What Is" of telling stories.*

Briefly consider a range of possible motives, including the expressions of fear or longing, needs such as needing control, attention, recognition (validation) or, perhaps, needing to be rescued (as in co-dependence). Likewise, we can be powerfully motivated to avoid risks and responsibility. Bear in mind, I have suggested that we are not necessarily conscious of our motives in telling stories; rather, this is a question that is worth exploring.

TRUE STORIES

Assertions such as "This is a true story" and "I'm just being honest" form aspects of the "What Is Not" of storytelling. Such assertions often represent demands that the story be accepted at face value, and, quite possibly, the story-teller has an underlying agenda. Defining the story as "true," one way or another, can serve to preclude a challenge and correspondingly to assert the agenda. While this is certainly not necessarily the case, it is worth being alert to the possibility. *How we take that possibility into account is an aspect of the "What Is" of storytelling.*

At a less problematic level, stating that a story is true may simply be a claim that the events reported actually took place. What is obscured is the frame of reference that shapes the story. No matter how it is told, the story itself is necessarily a definition of events. There are many possible definitions. *Getting in touch with whatever underpins a story can help us attend to the "What Is" of how we are making sense of both the story and how it is told.*

SUMMARY

The "What Is Not" of our stories is the definition we apply to life experiences as well as to the layers of meanings that have already piled up around those experiences. To the extent we take on those definitions, we achieve a sense of certainty and identity. However, we do so at the risk of binding ourselves into an unnecessarily rigid view of our lives, of who we are and of the nature of the world around us. In doing so, we can generate a great deal of distress. On the other hand, *being aware of the "What Is" in telling our stories can take us into a wholly different realm.*

"WHAT IS" – HOW WE TELL OUR STORIES

There are many ways to tell our stories. How we tell our stories is the "What Is," the experiential aspect of the telling. Bear in mind that we tell ourselves stories in our heads as well as to other people. Both matter.

By being aware of the "What Is" of telling our stories, we are empowered to choose how we tell them, and we can predict how other people are likely to experience the telling. Here are several ways we may examine how we tell our stories.

Roles: *Perhaps the easiest way to identify how we distress ourselves is by identifying the role we play in the story. Here is a sampling of roles: Achiever, "The Boss," Connoisseur, Cop, a Failure, Fighter, Fixer, Hero, Judge, Student, Teacher, Victim – add more... . It may not be obvious why some of those roles, such as "Hero" are likely to generate distress for us. When we take on a role, ego generally requires us to live up to that claim. We can experience distress both in the demands of living up to a self-definition, as well as by castigating ourselves when we do not.*

Personal Qualities: *Alternatively, we can identify the qualities we seek to display or downplay in how we tell our stories. These qualities, positive and negative, include brave, capable, conscientious, helpful, helpless, loving, persistent, reliable, respectful, sensible, sensitive... the list goes on. Such qualities are closely allied with roles. They simply represent another way of identifying how we tell our stories.*

Feelings: *There are likely to be feeling states associated with telling our stories. Being aware of our feelings helps identify how we are telling our stories. Feelings include anger, anxiety, bored, depressed, desperate, envious, exalted, inspired, jealous, overwhelmed, resentful, and worried.*

Distress-Inducing Dynamics: *Finally, we can identify the dynamics of how we tell our stories. Dynamics include argumentative, exaggerating, catastrophizing, denying, lying (comes in many shades, including lying by omission), minimizing, promoting (including self-aggrandizement) and side-tracking (avoiding).*

Agenda: *A somewhat separate consideration is to notice if we have an agenda in telling our stories. Having an agenda means we want something from the other person, but we do not make it explicit or negotiate it. For instance, we might expect their co-operation on a project, and they are "in trouble" if they do not agree. We are not necessarily aware of having an agenda, but we know soon enough when we are disappointed. Getting in touch with our agenda and negotiating it with the other person attends to this issue, provided we are respectful of the other person's choices.*

TELLING STORIES, CULTIVATING BENEFIT

How can we tell stories and cultivate benefit? Start by being aware of our intention. Here the focus is on the broad intention to cultivate benefit. Cultivating benefit includes enhancing mutual understanding and appreciation, releasing disturbing emotions and thinking, healing relationships, the respectful setting of boundaries, and opening to an inclusive understanding of all that is.

Stories can range from a brief encounter at work today to deeply personal material from childhood. Being aware of our reasons and, in so far as possible, of our motivations allows us to monitor them and ensure that how we tell stories is congruent with mutual benefit.

With that backdrop in place, we may tell our stories in a few complementary ways. I will outline these ways as if we are the storyteller, but they apply equally well to how we listen.

One way is to tell our stories with appreciation. "Appreciation" includes telling them with compassion or perhaps with joy as well as with a more direct sense of valuing. In this process, we can open to empathy, beauty, and the daily miracle of life.

In referring to empathy, I intend "empathy" as an experience of mutuality wherein the listener both understands from the speaker's perspective and shows this understanding to the speaker. The speaker has the direct experience that the listener "gets it."

We also achieve a deeper self-understanding and self-acceptance when we tell our stories with appreciation. We notice, for example, a tendency to exaggerate or, perhaps, a need for the other person's approval. Bringing compassion to our inclinations, we can either acknowledge them directly or release them internally. In doing either, we shift to reflecting the amazingness that we are alive.

Even small incidents, such as spilling a cup of coffee, can be told in this way. How might a story about spilling a cup of coffee reflect "amazingness"? It is a matter of how we tell it. So often our stories are about something "being wrong" or about some sort of achievement. Alternatively, we can relate spilling the coffee with appreciation by alluding to the shining brown ripples of falling coffee and sensing the sting as it hits our thigh. In this way, everything becomes alive.

Another way of telling our stories with a beneficial intention is that of "exploration." It is telling as a way of discovering our own experience and meanings in the process of telling the story. For example, I may be generally aware as to why I see another person as attractive, but to tell a friend about this, I have to go deeper into self-understanding to give a coherent account of what I am relating.

Exploration may include:

- *being conscious of the role you are taking in telling the story.*

- *qualities you want to show or avoid showing.*

- *reasons and motives for telling the story. You may or may not actually choose to share this information explicitly.*

- *exploring the meanings, beliefs, and other associations you hold.*

- *identifying the implications of the story and how you are telling it for your well-being as well as that of the listener.*

- *and considering the question, "How does the story fit into a larger picture of your life or your understanding of the world?"*

In principle, we can find in any story, even a brief account of putting gas in the car, many of the elements suggested above. How far you want to go in exploring stories will vary, but it is always a choice. Bearing in mind that this book is about cultivating Discriminating Wisdom, peace of mind and a sense of inner freedom, then attending to how we tell our stories makes a difference. Practice #12 focuses our attention on this approach to telling stories.

Practice #12
Conscious Storytelling

Practice telling stories (and hearing them) consciously with appreciation and/ or exploration. Here are some questions you might ask of yourself:

1. What sort of Self am I creating with this story and the way I am telling it?

2. What am I doing (trying to do) in my telling of this story?

3. How can I cultivate appreciation in telling this story? (Appreciation is explored in detail in Contrast #19.)

4. How can I take this as an opportunity to explore at the same time as Cultivating peace of mind and a sense of inner freedom?

CONTRAST #13

EGO-IDENTITY and RIGIDITY contrasted with *CURIOSITY*

Most young children are naturally curious. They want to find out about the world, and about themselves in particular. Finding out includes asking what something is called, how things work and why things are the way they are. We can easily imagine a three-year-old looking at the night sky and asking, "Why are stars?"

Over the years, curiosity is replaced with knowledge and beliefs. Depending substantially on your socialization as a child you will hold a vast range of knowledge and beliefs with varying degrees of rigidity. For instance, your beliefs around "who you are" as a separate being are, for most people, rigid. Perhaps, you have no doubt who you are. You may find there is some fraying around the edges, perhaps doubts about whether you are really committed to a sustainable environment especially when you want a new car, but your core identity is solid. It matters not whether it is negative or positive or even racked with self-doubt; each person carries strong beliefs about "this is the way I am."

Curiosity, on the other hand, tends to get restricted to a limited number of domains as we grow up. Think about yourself now: what are you genuinely curious about? Perhaps you have particular interests in health and medicine. What about sexual curiosity? Or is there some area of study or professional application in which you invest your energy? Perhaps you really appreciate other cultures and like to travel. The range of possible domains is wide. Yet the number you are actively interested in is perhaps quite limited. As a broader consideration, what is your overall sense of curiosity? Can you say with certainty that you approach day-to-day life with a spirit of inquiry?

WHAT IS NOT – THE RIGIDITY OF EGO-IDENTITY

In this contrast, we are concerned with the rigidity of ego-identity, "The Self," and the beneficial consequences of getting curious about that "Self."

Whatever constitutes your ego-identity defines how you relate both to the world and with the on-going flow of your immediate experience - sensual, emotional, and mental. To the extent that peace of mind and an inner sense of freedom are what you are seeking, it is your ego-identity combined with brain functioning that oppose those intentions.

In earlier Contrasts, we examined core beliefs (Contrast #5), Ego-Involvement (Contrast #6) and Truth and Reality (Contrast #9) as well as Resistance (Contrast #3). These contrasts speak to the solidity and power of our beliefs about "who we are."

We can get in touch with the rigidity of our ego, for example, by observing ourselves arguing or becoming defensive. Earlier I asserted that our identities are constructed upon a foundation of beliefs. They are not fixed, not The Truth. This assertion may seem like nonsense when we are caught up in the throes of ego-involvement. At these times, it seems impossible that things could be any other way.

On the other hand, there will be times, indeed periods of time, when your thinking is flexible, and you are open-minded. Rigidity is not an issue at those times. Open, receptive awareness does not generate distress. Rather, the rigidity of the ego shows up situationally. When we are worried for instance, we can be totally consumed.

The fluidity of open-mindedness is quickly displaced by the solidity of ego-involvement. This rigidity shows up in default mode thinking (Contrast #4), as well as in our actions and interactions. Yet most of the time, we do not even notice that we are enacting our ego-identity.

A simple clue to ego-involvement and rigidity is found in noticing when we make judgments. For instance, notice liking as, "I like this... ," "I don't like that... ." Even in liking and disliking, you are in the thick of ego-involvement, and it gets thicker in difficult times. Many people experience this as an underlying sense of dissatisfaction. We tend to remember this negativity and use it use as a lens through which we view aspects of our lives.

"WHAT IS" – CURIOSITY

The cultivation of curiosity is a re-awakening of a natural capacity, as I described in introducing this contrast. I defined curiosity as "What Is" in that we experience what we call "curiosity" directly, for instance, as an urge to find out. Pause for a moment. Can you get that sense of "wanting to find out" right now? "What might it be?" We can be curious about anything, from the spelling of a particular word to "Why stars?"

This contrast is focused on getting curious about how we trap ourselves within the rigidity of our ego-identity. *As we invoke curiosity towards being ego-involved, we are laying a path to becoming free. To switch the metaphor, curiosity becomes the lubricant that frees up the rigidity of our ego-identity. Bear in mind, our egos operate to define how things are or should or should not be. "Things" include ourselves, other people, and anything else you care to name that you desire, push away, or avoid.*

Noticing both desire and pushing away, including avoidance, can be reframed as opportunities to get curious. However, "getting curious" may be the last thing you want to do – after all, "If you don't like it, you don't like it and that is that!" Or is it? You have the power to make this a moment of choice. You can take the easy, well-worn path, such as complaining about whatever it is you do not like. Or you can explore as, "How come I don't like cold brussels sprouts?" Or, more significantly, "How come I do not like being told I'm 'not with it'?"

It may seem totally obvious why you do not like be treated with disrespect. Do not allow that "obviousness" to sidetrack you. Invoking curiosity is seeking to understand how you came to get hooked in the first place. You make attending to how you are treated a separate matter.

*This process involves **shifting out of** getting caught up in a loop:*

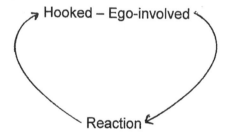

*and **shifting into** separating ego-involvement from whatever is at issue:*

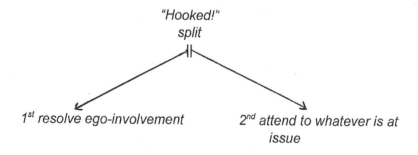

For this practice to work, we need to get curious about becoming ego-involved. We start by recognizing that we have become "hooked!" Now explore. Seek to understand your own propensities and vulnerabilities and identify the beliefs that bind you. We achieve some resolution by attending to underlying needs in beneficial ways (See Practice #13 below).

As we make this shift, we are gradually freed from getting caught up in our ego. As experience of freedom increases, our sense of distress decreases. We are, in effect, training ourselves to act in a principled way; for example, by acting for the well-being of all. With such guidance, we are not acting to protect or promote the small sense of self, our ego-identity.

You may not feel curious, or you may resist cultivating curiosity. Either way, get curious about what is going on for you. Bear in mind, you are not being asked to give up anything that is beneficial for you. You are being asked to explore what keeps you confined to your old, circular path of ego-involvement, and to lay a new path guided by curiosity.

For example, parents who want their children to excel enroll their children in many programs. Both the parents and the children get stressed keeping up with the schedule. The parents who insist on high standards and persistence are going to have vastly different outcomes from *another set of parents who recognize the stress that everyone is feeling. They get curious about what they have been hooked into. They discover, perhaps through taking a parenting course or attending counselling, what a complex web of factors constrained them to act in the way they did. They shift their priorities. Now, they are putting everyone's emotional well-being and engagement with the activities that interest them first.*

*To cultivate curiosity, you may want to revisit Contrast #3, discussing "Resistance," and Contrast #5, particularly in respect to "Exploring." One way around blocks to curiosity is to use the magic of "If." Ask yourself, "**If** I was curious about getting hooked, what would I be curious about?" See what answer bubbles up. Allow that this is a practice. You are generating new dendritic connections in the brain when you pursue novel lines of thinking. It takes time and effort to cultivate curiosity in areas that have been sealed off for years, let alone work through any resistance from your ego-identity.*

Practice #13
Cultivating Curiosity

Cultivate curiosity by:

1. **Notice getting hooked** – Name it, "Hooked!"

2. **Breathe** – Set aside the urge to react to the hook. You may wish to note the content in writing as reassurance that you will not get forget it.

3. **Cultivate curiosity** – As examples: "If I was curious, what would I want to know?" "How come I got hooked?" "What does this tell me about myself?" "What must I believe to react in this way?" "How do I know?" The answers can help you deepen self-understanding.

4. **Releasing the hook** – Assuming the hook is around an unmet need, "What is getting hooked in this way telling me I need?" "How can I attend to that need in a beneficial way?"

CONTRAST #14

"EITHER/OR" contrasted with *"BOTH ... AND"*

The perspective of "either/or" occurs as we define our options as mutually exclusive. Either you agree with me, or you don't. Certainly, there are times that mutually exclusive thinking is entirely valid. When I fly in a plane, either we will land safely or be involved in a crash or trouble of some sort. On the other hand, we often get caught up in a perspective of "either/or" creating arguments, both with other people and within our own thinking. All too often it is our perspectives that are creating mutual exclusivity, not some circumstance beyond our control.

Our perspective creating the "either/or" is a limitation of our mode of thought, no matter that our minds insist that we have no other choice. As a result, we keep ourselves stuck in difficult circumstances, such as unhappy jobs. Similarly, "either/or" thinking bedevils many close relationships, so that when we can shift our perspective to "both ... and", our options may open up.

"WHAT IS NOT" – EITHER/OR

When we take an "either/or" perspective, we present ourselves with a stark choice; for instance, "either we get married or I'm out of here." "Either/or" is worth considering at the broad level of how we generally engage in living our lives. Second, we will examine how we might encounter specific situations.

Consider how we can erode or corrode our quality of life in general. For instance, to what extent and in what ways do we engage with life as unsatisfactory? Dissatisfaction has many manifestations, such as looking at things critically as not good enough, stressing over what might happen, and needing to improve present circumstances. These views represent an "either/or" perspective in which things are so obviously not what they should or could be.

Experientially, we may not even notice that we are hung up in "either/or." Essentially, we are caught in the belief, "**Either** things are the way I want them to be, **or** there is something amiss." "Well," you say indignantly, "They should be, and they are not, damn it!" Your indignation, if you happened to react, or dissatisfaction in general derives directly from beliefs about how things ought to be. We react to our beliefs, "What Is Not," and they override the "What Is" of our immediate experience.

We also encounter specific situations that we define in "either/or" terms. *It may well be worth asking the question, "Is this my perspective in action or are there really no other possibilities?" These situations include work and personal relationships, recreational and intellectual interests as well as beliefs about ourselves and other people. Similarly, when we find ourselves framing issues as right/wrong, good/bad, desirable/undesirable, we can take these occasions as opportunities to identify the assumptions we are making. When we find ourselves being categorical, it is usually worth reflecting on the perspective we have adopted rather than jumping to conclusions.*

Dwelling in "either/or" is generally limiting and often induces distress. However, we do not want to dismiss the "either/or" perspective blindly. It can be useful in certain circumstances, and there are also situations that are "trivial." Both are worth noting.

Either/or can be useful in risk assessment. For instance, it does not matter if the concern is that you are short of time in getting to an appointment or considering making a major investment. Either you will be on time, or you will be late; either the investment will increase in value, or its value will stay the same or go down.

Are you prepared to accept the risk and deal with the fallout? If not, do not do it. Notice that the key question here is recognizing what is actually within your control and what is not. Attend to what is within your control – drive carefully even if doing so makes you late; attend to what ensues if an issue arises from having been late.

Any situation in which there is a *de facto* correct answer is "trivial." Adding a column of numbers, as in a bank account, is a prime example. There is only one correct total. When an objective determination is possible, then do not argue from an ego-involved perspective; "I'm right," for instance. Rather, test the correctness of the solution proposed.

"WHAT IS" – BOTH ... AND

Here I want to draw attention to being caught in the immediate experience of "either/or" and making it an opportunity to take a "both ... and" perspective. There is a significant difference between, for instance, conflicting positions, "**Either** I am right, **or** he is right," *and the recognition of difference,* "We are **both** right in our own mind **and** are difference." *This allows the possibility of resolving the issue to their mutual satisfaction. Shifting our thinking from "either/or" to "both ... and" can be quite demanding on our creativity. We also need to be willing to set aside our preconceptions or do so at least for the time being to allow the adoption of a "both ... and" perspective.*

*"Both ... and" acknowledges **both** how we are engaging with any particular circumstance **and** how we are choosing to attend to it. As a simple illustration, I may notice I feel upset that I am late for a meeting – that is okay; experientially that is "What Is." I can release feeling upset, instead of reacting. If being late requires remedial work, I will attend to that when the need arises. Actually allowing ourselves to take the risk of consequences may well require considerable personal work before we feel even reasonably at ease taking this step.*

Note that "acknowledging how we are engaging" represents a radically distinct perspective from that of, "What is right? Or "Wrong?" or "What needs to be fixed or improved?" What we choose to do about our experience allows that we have a degree of agency in most situations, and implicitly, we are accepting that there are limitations to what we can do. Although, surely, what we can and cannot do, and for that matter what we are willing to do, vary situationally.

The columns below illustrate a range of applications of this contrast. It is not intended to be exhaustive, and the illustrations may well overlap. The intention is to alert the reader to opportunities to shift from "either/or" to "both ... and." In defining such occasions as "opportunities," I am recommending that we attend open-heartedly to our real time experience. Try it out. Where does creating the perspective of opportunity serve you in the quest to cultivate benefit?

The particular "either/or" dilemmas illustrated will apply to some people but not to everyone. Rather, if you find you are caught in an "either/or" dilemma, identify which type fits for you, and slot in the elements that constitute the "either/or."

*Notice that "both ... and" entails a shift from default thinking to directly applying metacognitive abilities, looking in on what you are doing either with your thinking or socially as you interact with other people. The shift involves **both** recognizing "This is what is going on" **and** addressing the question, "How do I handle this situation to cultivate benefit?"*

1. We may be ambivalent about a relationship:

Either I stay in this relationship, **Or** I leave it.	*What shifts would I have to make to **both** stay in the relationship **and** feel good about staying?* *Alternatively, what shifts would I have to make to **both** leave **and** feel good about leaving?*

2. In disagreements, such as arguing over who is right:

Taking the position "I am right" has an implicit "**either** I'm right **or** you are." We generally defend our positions.	*We still take positions. We recognize that **both** of us are right from within our own frames of reference **and** we are different. "How do we address the difference?"*

3. Trust is an issue, not when it has not been compromised. But rather the question arises out of fear and uncertainty:

Either you trust me, **or** you don't. This dichotomy could arise from an underlying need for certainty. The downside is that when trust is held in question, we will tend to notice what we deem to be untrustworthy.	*Act to **both** cultivate trustworthiness, as a mutual process **and** recognize limitations.* *Trustworthiness is always going to be circumscribed in one way or another – what counts as "trustworthy" varies from person to person. Also, the context, such as the type of relationship, is a major consideration.*

Another class of "either/or" dilemmas are generated by how we think.

4. Anxiety shows up in many forms depending upon our socialization and how our identity is constructed around our core beliefs.

Either I am safe, **or** I have an intimate relationship. Another example: **either** I matter, **or** I must give myself away to please my partner. **Either** I do what I am supposed to do (internalized expectations) **or** I'm a failure (or, any other negative forms of self-image, such as selfish, shame-worthy etc.). **Either** I worry about 'this', **or** things will go terribly wrong.	*I can be **both** safe **and** be in an intimate relationship This integration will probably carry a sense of risk. It becomes useful to explore taking risks with situationally appropriate caution and consider counselling.* ***Both** practice and release the internal pressure to conform, **and** I choose to invest myself in what matters to me independently of preconceived expectations.* *I will **both** practice releasing worry whenever it pops up (default thinking - Contrast #4) **and** follow through on my plan (see Contrast #8).*

5. **Criticalness,** as I use the word here, is intended to cover a full range of negative thoughts and judgments about ourselves and other people, from "What a dumb thing to do," to the extreme, "They don't deserve to live." No matter whether criticism is self-directed or projected onto other people, the effects are broadly similar, namely physiological arousal, emotional distress, and the reinforcement of self-defeating beliefs.

Either I am justified in my criticism, **or** I have got it all wrong. I believe I am right, no matter that the opinion is negative, even self-destructive. The belief is so powerful that "Or" is seldom even noticed.	***Both** recognize "I am being critical" (you may prefer another category, such as "judgmental" or "negative;" choose a word that works for you), **and** "I see what I need is ... ." Ensure "the need" is framed to benefit the longer term, such as, "I need to allow myself to be at peace in my mind."*

6. "Categorical Imperatives" are a class of beliefs that assert that things are a particular way. This class may well embody all the previous points. However, they can be readily identified by noticing when we make use of particular words, and that is the point I want to draw your attention to here.

"Either/Or"	"Both ... And
"This ... **must** happen." "This ... **always** happens "This ... **never** happens." "This ... is a **fact**," implying the claim made is **True**, representing absolute Reality. The **"or"** may not be articulated.	*Both recognize your investment in the opinion and consider your options in what you do with the opinion.*

CONCLUSION

When we observe, we will find ourselves caught up in either/or thinking more often than we might recognize at first glance. Certainly, there are situations in which our choices are limited to either/or, and there are others in which we can make constructive use of "either/or," as in, "It looks like I'm going to be late for the meeting." No point in rousing anxiety. Either "I'll be late, or I won't. I may as well be at ease." Alternatively, by being alert to the inclusive "both/and" perspective, we may be able to open many unexpected opportunities.

Practice #14
Shifting "Either/Or" to "Both ... And"

1. Notice when your mind set is "It's this way." That is it! No alternative, at least not for me. This is the hidden sense of either/or.

2. Notice also when you think of a situation as being "Either the way **or** that," where you have no sense of having other options. (Some situations do not allow other options. These are not so frequent as it may seem). It may be that we do not like the obvious alternatives and taking an "either/or" position lets us off the hook.

3. Shift to meta-cognition – look in on the either/or bind. **Both** identify what in your thinking is binding you into being caught in taking an either/or position, **and**

4. Identify and attend to the need underlying the bind. How can you attend to that need in a way likely to bring about a beneficial outcome?

CONTRAST #15

POWER contrasted with *LOVE*

This contrast lays out a conceptual distinction between "Power" and *Love.*" The following Contrast, #16, provides fully developed example of power as expressed in Games and *love as represented by Play.*

The practice is to recognize which aspect of this contrast we are enacting in the moment. This is totally apart from the content of a situation, the content being what we define as going on. When we recognize and accept that we are exercising power over, we can evaluate whether that is a position we wish to take. Likewise, expressing *love* is not always appropriate either. Several of the pros and cons of each are set out in the concluding section of this contrast.

THE "WHAT IS NOT" OF POWER

Power is approached here as "Power Over" another person, people, a situation. To clarify, when I refer to power as being "What Is Not," I am not suggesting that "power" does not exist in terms of both its generation, and its exercise. The authority of the legal system, ranging from policing to decisions by the Supreme Court are prototypical of institutions that are invested with wide ranging powers aimed at retaining social control, rather euphemistically called "maintaining the peace."

This type of power tends to govern our lives both daily and personally. "Power over" is exercised and all too frequently contested within couples, families and between friends, in work situations and sometimes with strangers. We can also distress ourselves with internal struggles over power and, likewise, powerlessness. As an example, we may feel a driving need to be "in charge." On the other hand, we might feel deep shame if we see ourselves as being weak.

"Power over" depends on our capacity to define the situation, person, relationship and so forth. This is exemplified in recognizing that when one member of a relationship defines that relationship, then he or she controls it.

There are just a few criteria that distinguish Power and *Love,* both conceptually and in practice. These differences are tabulated below.

"WHAT IS" – LOVE

Love, as it is conceived here, is the polar opposite to Power. This contrast starts with Power being easy to conceive and define. *Whereas trying to define Love requires some imagination. Thinking metaphorically by referring to gardening may be helpful. The gardener loves both the garden and gardening. This gardener endeavors to ensure that the garden flourishes. Perhaps that is the essence.*

It is so that the gardener exercises Power in the garden. The gardener weeds and prunes and shapes and reshapes beds. Shaping, planting, and uprooting are on-going. **What is crucial is to recognize that here Power *is exercised in the service of Love.***

If we recognize that distinction, we can also recognize when Love is in service to Power. This is exemplified, in a broad sense, when one person both loves their partner and accepts being obedient to that partner.

POWER	LOVE
Defines – (see: Contrast #1) Every definition depends on making a distinction between "this" and "something else," as in, "You should've been home an hour ago!"	*Describes* – *(See: Contrast #1) Essentially description shows* **how** *the elements of the description are connected, as in "I feel so glad to see you."*
Any distinction generates separation.	*In the statement "… so glad to see …" represents how "I" feel connected with "you."*

Separation – Each distinction creates separation. This is an exercise of power. All too easily this creates separation between people. This is generally accepted and functional, as in many work environments. Clashes over the exercise of power account for wars on the battlefield and in the home.

Connection – *Descriptive language emphasizes the verb – whatever connects the subject, in the example above "I," with the object, in this case, "you" and "... glad to see... ." describes the nature of my present time connection with you.*

Love language always provides either connection or the avenue for connection.

Past-Future – Power is exercised by shaping the story of the past to serve the present exercise of power in our endeavor to define how the future will manifest. Notice the circularity in that process.

Now (Present Time) – *Love is expressed, experienced, and sustained in the moment. In that sense, the existence of Love is tenuous, and yet the possibility of continuity is, in principle, born every moment.*

Restricts Opportunities – The exercise of power over necessarily restricts opportunities. The power-holder determines what may or may not occur. The aim of Power is to determine the outcome. Not to achieve the expected outcome is likely to be deemed to be a failure.

Opens Opportunities –*A key aspect that reflects the amorphous nature of Love is that Love necessarily opens to opportunities. In opening opportunities, one is not seeking to predetermine what unfolds. Staying in the modality of Love implies that one is open to outcomes.*

Imagine a couple on the verge of separating. One, taking a Power perspective, says, "We took a vow to have and to hold until death do us part. No, I will not give you a divorce." Even rights and freedoms granted in a nation's constitution will be found to constrain citizens to behave in particular ways. Only within those parameters is one free to move. That dynamic applies at all levels of societal organization. Within families, there may be competition over who is in control. Within oneself, self-definition, as in "I am such a loser," may define the individual in such a way that he or she gives up trying. Less obvious is the person with the self-image, "I'm a go-getter." The capacity to define permits the exercise of Power.

Imagine a couple on the verge of separating. One, taking a Love perspective, says, "I feel distraught. Can we explore the possibility of reconciliation?"

It is not that outcomes do not matter. Rather it is, coming from a loving perspective, that we recognize and accept it is quite possible that we will not get the outcome we desire.

To the extent families, couples and personal relationships are conducted from a loving perspective, any exercise of power will be firmly in the service of Love

Closed Communication – Communication from the power-holder to the recipient is substantially top-down (unilateral). The recipient might advocate for rights, for instance, but depending upon the power-holder's capacity to exercise power, the power-holder determines what is done with the supplicant's request or demand.

The language of Power is predominantly definitional. Overall, this language is simpler and briefer than the *expression of Love.*

Open Communication – *Adopting a Love perspective, power is shared, as in making decisions. Likewise, communication is bilateral (multi-lateral), requires an elevated level of communicative skills, which may have to be learned and will need to be put into practice.*

These skills include: an invitational style, maintaining mutual respect, an advanced capacity to recognize each other's perspective and to work with these perspectives reciprocally. Also, the skills to reconcile differences and negotiate "win-win" decisions.

I am primarily concerned that these ideas serve to benefit us, individually, and in our personal relationships. If we are to have rewarding lives, *Love* is surely the dominant perspective we want to adopt. We do have a choice. Then most of the time, Power needs to be in service to *Love*. There are exceptions. Perhaps the most obvious is in life-threatening situations. It may well be that with the house on fire one person takes charge in the name of Love. "No. Stay here. You can't go back and get Kitty!"

In turning to Contrast #16, Games contrasted with *Play,* we explore a prototypical exemplar of Power in Games, and *Love in Play.*

Practice 15
Cultivating Awareness of Power and Love

1. Observe yourself while you are relating with another person:

   a. Am I relating in terms of Power or in terms of Love? (You could apply the criteria listed in the columns above to check.)

   b. Am I relating "Power only," "Love only," "Power in the service of Love," or "Love in the service of Power"?

2. Choose how you want to continue communicating (relating).

CONTRAST #16

GAMES contrasted with *PLAY*

"WHAT IS NOT" – GAMES

Games constitute "What Is Not." They are brought into being through processes of definition. What is defined are particular ways of interacting. The prototypical game is played by numbers of people forming opposing sides according to a set of rules that include setting the number of players on both sides, a method of scoring, what counts as winning, the duration of the game and so forth. The fundamental distinction that marks a **game** is to bring it to an end by winning.

Let me draw your attention to the point that we engage in much of our life as if it is a game. We work wanting to get tasks completed. We relate with other people competitively by asserting our opinion over someone else's, or for instance, deciding who does what around the house.

Make a point of looking at your day-to-day activities from a "games" perspective while you are engaged in doing them. You will probably notice that you create the day as a series of episodes. Time for breakfast, time to check emails and so forth.

We set up rules for ourselves and our relationships. These rules are for the most part so ordinary that we barely notice them. They usually only come to the fore when we transgress them. Having lunch may be a simple example. Do you watch what you eat? If you satisfy your expectations, you come out a winner. If you didn't, you lost and perhaps get down on yourself. Some "games" are played with only one side making the rules, too often with brutal consequences.

In a relational situation, imagine that you are out to dinner with your partner, and you disagree over the quality of the food. Out of that argument comes a winner and a loser. Or perhaps it is a draw, and you retire to separate rooms, emotionally bloodied and bruised. That is a view of life as a series of interpersonal games. This goes on at larger and larger scales. Political activities, as well as our society in general, operate much in this way.

You may think I have taken the idea of games too far. Perhaps you want to use the term only about certain kinds of sports. If so, set that restriction (resistance) aside. The value of considering life as a series of games is that you can make this into an opportunity to reflect on whether this is how you want to engage.

The upside of participating in the games of life is that you usually know the rules, and you can decide whether you want to participate in particular games. Correspondingly, you can also decide what rules you are going to break and what risks you are prepared to take. At least you do not need to participate blindly.

The major downside is that you are not living your own life. Whether you are a football player or a scrabble player, husband or wife, boss or employee is moot. You are still following rules. You are still living in the context of "a rule book," no matter whether you follow the rules or not.

All is not lost! You have a choice. You might want to explore living playfully.

"WHAT IS" – PLAY

PLAY

Play is defined here as any activity undertaken entirely for its own sake with the intention of keeping it going. Undertaking an activity for its own sake implies we are immersed in the immediacy of present-time experience. Implicitly or explicitly, we engage with the question, "How do I keep this going?"

Some activities, such as having a conversation with a friend, can be entirely play. Notice that the intention to keep play going entails being sensitive to whoever is involved, including oneself.

Imagine that this play is between two friends. They have thoroughly enjoyed exploring ideas and sharing each other's understandings. Mutual sensitivity allows that they have enjoyed this time together. Either or both have other matters to attend to. However, the intention to keep play going still applies. Affirming mutual appreciation and, for instance, arranging when next to meet allows for continuity of play as a series of episodic experiences. Notice that there is nothing they are trying to bring to an end. Rather, there is an interlude between episodes of play.

Long ago Ram Dass made a comment to the effect, "If anyone is willing to come out and play, treasure the opportunity. But you have no right to force anyone to play." This comment is worth attending to. We can invite people to play but insisting on playing turns play into a game. We make it into a game in that we win or lose depending on whether or not we are successful in persuading the other person to do something against their will.

Opportunities for unsullied play may not be frequent. However, we can engage in many of our endeavors playfully.

ENGAGING PLAYFULLY

Engaging playfully is attending to a task with all the actions performed light-heartedly. "Light-hearted performance" will be detailed in a moment. This matters because being able to address serious matters with an easy heart is conducive to personal well-being and to a reduction of anxiety and distress.

It is possible to approach much of life playfully. A living example of this way of engaging is the 14th Dalai Lama. Even in serious times, it is possible to hold events and many emotions with a lighter heart and be fully present even to the woundedness of challenging times. For instance, the Dalai Lama has referred to the Chinese as, "My friends the enemy... ."

Perhaps thinking of the Dalai Lama is setting the bar high. We do not need to impose excessive demands upon ourselves. Consider engaging in ordinary day-to-day affairs playfully, or at least more playfully than at present. Why do so?

Overall, we tend to be serious in our activities. It does not matter that we laugh. If we are not already treating the matter seriously, often there is surface laughter but underneath lies a sea of seriousness.

As a culture, we take life very seriously. This attitude is normalized. Perhaps we do not even consider it. Certainly, there are many other matters that warrant our full attention. That we have much to attend to is a different matter from treating many daily events seriously. We bring the attitude of seriousness to the events. It is not a quality that is inherent to those events.

While it is likely that seriousness is built upon the survival benefit of our inherited negativity, we distress ourselves way beyond anything that is needful. But taking things seriously is not fixed. *When we examine our seriousness, we find that we have a strong ego-investment in most of what we take seriously.*

Since seriousness represents a mindset, it is within our capacity to shift to a lighter way of engaging with life events. A prime example of doing so is reflected in the injunction usually meted out to children, "Don't cry over spilt milk." Since most people get upset when something goes wrong, we can beneficially practice this piece of wisdom.

Engaging playfully begins with holding any activity in a broad perspective. No matter what it is, in the timescale of evolution, it is minute; in the vastness of the galaxies, it is minute. But it is what we have in the moment. Can we see the preciousness of that moment? Even as our lives get swallowed up, so does the moment. This very transience can be held as precious, but not held onto.

As soon as we hold onto an experience, or push it away, or deny its existence, we create distress. *When we embrace both its presence and its transience, we are engaging lightly, appreciating it for what it is and moving on.*

Besides widening our perspective, we can engage with humor. We can see both our human-ness and our circumstances with a twist such that the ordinary becomes extraordinary. We create a sense of surprise. This idea is expressed in Mark Twain's comment printed in 1897 in response to a newspaper report of his death. He completed his statement writing, "The report my death was an exaggeration."

Another way of engaging playfully is to look for and focus on generating beauty in the moment. There is no comparing here, no judgment. *In effect, we are engaging through the question, "What can I appreciate in this moment?" "Appreciation" is explored in Contrast #19.*

Where comparison and judgment create separation, *playfulness and appreciation are the realization of connection. We can appreciate soap bubbles in the washing-up water as much as being amazed at the corpse in an open casket. We can be ever-present to our immediate experience – playfully.*

In this way we can treat even serious considerations as mattering without weighing them down by making them important. When we examine this "importance," we find that it is largely a matter of self-importance and ego-involvement, even though the last thing we want to do is to admit that. This is not to say that they do not matter. Not attending to failing bolts in a bridge could lead to a disaster. That we attend to what needs attention makes a differ-ence, and how we attend to it also makes a difference. By paying attention to how we attend, we can create an opportunity to shift from the seriousness of a game to the light-heartedness of play.

In playing and engaging playfully we foster caring and compassion. This comes about because we are engaging experientially and, thus we are connected instead of being separated by imposing our definitions and judgments.

Attending to how we engage with events requires practice. Cultivating appreciation and curiosity provides the means. We enter a direct, experiential relationship with that which we explore and appreciate. This approach enables us to divest ourselves of ego-identified engagement with events as they arise. We can learn to reframe negative experiences as "useful." They alert us to being ego-attached. This point is addressed in the next contrast, #17.

Practice #16.1
An Exercise in Playfulness

Imagine you are on a hunt or are an explorer. Prowl around the house, or wherever you happen to be, for 5 to 10 minutes a day. Peer around corners and into half-concealed spaces like under furniture. Look to see what pops into sight next and next and next. Do not indulge yourself with commentary such as on the need for housework!

Practice #16.2
Entering Play, Fostering Playfulness

Note: This exercise is for safe situations. There is no immediate danger nor some unacceptable personal risk.

1. Notice being serious – taking things seriously. Do not explore how you are generating "seriousness" in this practice. That issue is covered in a number of other Contrasts, especially #17 & #18.

2. "What do I want to keep going here?" Find some aspect of your immediate experience that you value or enjoy. Do not accept "Nothing" as an answer. At the very least, we want to keep breathing. Value that!

3. Whatever you want to keep going, bring in lightness, compassion, appreciation and connection. Naming the process observed is one way to achieve this. Examples: flowers name as "flowering"; the sink overflowing, "flowing," and flushing the toilet bowl, "gurgling" and listen. We can play with pretty much anything when we are so minded.

CONTRAST #17

EGO-ATTACHMENT
contrasted with *NATURAL ATTACHMENT*

An aspect of *Discriminating Wisdom* is to distinguish ego-attachment from natural attachment. We benefit by attending to these two forms of attachment in distinct ways. Even though they co-arise, we still practice them differently.

The concept of attachment is the principle we are considering here. Experientially, we encounter them as feelings, emotions, and sensations in the body. All kinds of thoughts occur as we make associations in the brain. **However feelings, emotions and sensations give us the cues we need so that we can work with attachment.**

"WHAT IS NOT" – EGO-ATTACHMENT

We have considered ego-attachment from several different perspectives in earlier contrasts. All I want to do here is give a wide range of signs telling us that we have become ego-involved. There are a couple of ways of labelling the process. One is "getting hooked." The second is that we "glom onto" an idea, position, a feeling. Getting hooked is when a sign is taken as coming from the outside ("Signs" are discussed on p.6). Whereas we can see how we, individually, have glommed onto, for instance, our feelings, opinions, or a story about a particular situation and are building it up into a drama, for instance.

Let's work with the assumption that a need of some sort underlies every attachment. With that assumption in mind, upon recognizing we are hooked, *we first practice releasing, or* at least diminishing the attachments. *Then we identify the underlying need and endeavor to attend to it in ways likely to lead to benefit.*

This approach is vastly different from how we ordinarily handle getting hooked. Usually, we react in some way or another. For example, we may fly into a rage or avoid the whole issue and nurse resentment. Patterns of this sort are re-enactments of habits, and re-enacting habits strengthens both our habits and our attachments.

Signs we are ego-attached include a wide range of "negative" feelings and emotions. The list below identifies many of the feelings we are likely to encounter. The feelings marked with an asterisk(*) do not necessarily indicate ego-attachment. They may represent either or both natural attachment and ego-attachment. This implies that they can usefully be considered from both perspectives. Certainly, the other feelings may include aspects of natural attachment. This list is not intended as being The Truth. Rather, use it to identify possible cues for exploration.

FEELINGS SIGNALING EGO-ATTACHMENT:

Afraid *	Defeated	Exasperated	Infuriated
Aggressive*	Depressed *	Excited *	Intimidated *
Agonizing	Despair*	Fearful *	Irritable *
Angry	Determined*	Foolish	Isolated*
Annoyed	Disgusted*	Flustered	Jealous*
Anxious	Disregarded*	Frantic *	Jumpy
Apathetic	Disrespected *	Frightened *	Kind *
Apologetic	Disappointed	Frustrated *	Lazy*
Arrogant	Disapproving	Grief-stricken *	Left-out
Ashamed	Disbelieving *	Guilty	Lonely *
Bashful	Discouraged *	Helpful *	Loving *
Betrayed*	Disgusted*	Helpless	Love-struck
Blue	Disregarded*	Hopeful	Manic *
Bored*	Disrespected	Hopeless	Melancholic *
Burdened	Dissatisfied*	Hurt	Mischievous
Caring *	Distraught *	Hyper-vigilant	Miserable *
Cautious *	Disturbed *	(on guard)*	Moody *
Charmed	Dominated	Hysterical	Negative
Cheated	Driven*	Idiotic	Nervous*
Condemned	Embarrassed	Ignored*	Obstinate
Confident *	Empty	Imposed upon	Optimistic*
Conflicted *	Enraged	Impulsive *	Outraged
Confused *	Enthusiastic *	Indifferent *	Pained
Crushed	Envious	Indecisive *	Panicky*

Paranoid	Rejected*	Spiteful	Ugly
Perplexed *	Restless *	Stupid	Uncertain *
Persecuted*	Satisfied *	Surprised *	Unhappy*
Pressured	Scared*	Tense *	Uninterested *
Put-upon	Shame*	Terrified *	Unmotivated *
Puzzled *	Sheepish	Thwarted *	Vulnerable*
Rage *	Shocked	Trapped	Worried
Regretful	Smug	Troubled	Worthless

Other States Signaling Ego-Attachment – There are several behaviors that also signal ego-attachment. These include defensiveness, justifying (elaborated below), blaming, and criticizing, many forms of wanting and desiring, avoidance and denial.

I have frequently mentioned justification. I want to emphasize the point that much of our talk involves justifying, for instance, why we hold a particular opinion or why we "behaved like that." Even when we do not justify, we have justifications lurking close by, just in case we are questioned.

It can be helpful to recognize forms of justification. In recognizing what we are doing, we can make other choices. We can practice releasing attachments where we find that justification is self-defeating.

Justification includes: defensiveness, making excuses, explaining (especially in conflictual situations), lying, voicing opinions (frequently; not always), rationalization and stories (many; not all).

There are forms of explanation that may not represent ego-attachment. For instance, mechanical explanations, such as how a car works, and scientific explanations, say for global warming, serve as examples. Where this may become problematic is in being ego-attached to our explanations. Being attached in that way makes a great difference in how we conduct ourselves and for our self-regard. It is important to recognize that being ego-attached to "being right" differs categorically from the validity of the explanation for the phenomenon observed.

Being ego-attached is not a "bad thing." We encounter these attachments many times daily. It is what we do with our experiences of attachment that makes the difference. We have a choice between acting out the hook **or** engaging beneficially by applying *Discriminating Wisdom*.

"WHAT IS" – NATURAL ATTACHMENT

Natural attachment is experiential and is entailed in our nature as a species, whereas ego-attachment is triggered by thinking and belief. Conversely, natural attachment might be thought of as arising from biological processes in our bodies. These experiences are rewarding when needs are fulfilled, and they signal separation as loss or threat when we experience distress.

Obvious types of natural attachment include parent-child bonding and grief at a death, as well as sexuality, productivity, sustenance, comfort, and safety. Out of bonding we can recognize love, feelings of affection, affiliating with other people, and appreciation for the familiar, such as pets and nature. Sexuality adds other dimensions. Grief and sadness reflect loss of this kind of attachment.

We seem to have a natural attachment, or in this case a desire, to be productive and, by extension, to take risks. Although we become strongly ego-attached to the many forms of productivity and risk-taking, we also experience an intrinsic rewardingness (including shots of dopamine) both in doing the things we want to do and in their completion. We can certainly recognize survival benefits in "being productive" and risk-taking, albeit circumscribed by many and variable considerations. We also experience distress when we are required to do things that we do not want to do, and boredom when we have insufficient going on to engage our interest.

Security, in the sense of having sustenance and comfort, seems closely related. Sufficient food, warmth, cleanliness, and closeness to several people are all things we generally need, strive for, and find rewarding. They complement safety.

We generally seek safety. Even in taking risks, we will usually take precautions, especially in the context of high-risk sports, such as more advanced mountain climbing. If, on the other hand, risk-taking is bound up with our ego, we may dismiss natural fears or sense of threat in order to prove something. Taking into account what motivates us can be a valuable guide in the decisions we make. Indeed, this could represent the application of Discriminating Wisdom.

We can recognize our natural attachments through our feelings and emotions. There are a sizable number such feelings. Each one encompasses a range of intensity and nuance. The main emotions appear to be affiliation (caring, closeness, connection, belonging), disgust, enjoyment, excitement, fear, irritability, joy, rage, sadness (including grief) and startle (surprise). Although, unsurprisingly, most of these are experienced when combined with ego-attachment.

I say "appear to be" because there is no general agreement regarding natural, or universal, human emotions. The list I have offered is, let us say, serviceable. I can make an argument for each one being grounded in survival for us as a semi-social species. You may discover others for yourself that you can identify as distinct from ego-attachment.

You may well have noticed that feeling happy and love are not included. Happiness is addressed in Contrast #19. Think of love in the context of natural attachment as affiliation.

DISTINGUISHING EGO-ATTACHEMENT FROM NATURAL ATTACHMENT

The main point in this contrast is to discriminate ego-attachment from natural attachment. This is because, as mentioned previously, we want to practice them in separate ways. Engaging in such practices is an aspect of practicing Discriminating Wisdom.

1. ***Ego-attached feelings*** *– We benefit by releasing ego-attached feelings, rather than glomming onto them. With practice, we become increasingly free of the distress these feelings represent or induce.*

2. ***Feelings associated with natural attachment*** *– We want to fully embrace feelings associated with natural attachment. "Embrace" implies taking them in experientially and intentionally, even if they are difficult, as in grieving the loss of a close family member. On the other hand, do not hang on to them. Let them have their time and move on.*

We can recognize being ego-attached using specific cues. The idea of "hooked" can be used generically for all four categories of cues, and specifically as follows:

1. ***"Hooked"*** *– could also be identified as, "not liking," feeling defensive, turned off, tense, got a charge out of it, ... others? As mentioned earlier in this Contrast, we could also notice this as "glomming on" to a point of view or to a feeling; unwilling to examine our own attachment.*

2. ***"Driven"*** *– a sense of pressure or urge to act or to achieve certain goals. This may be sensed as "must do," or retrospectively, "I had to... ." These are feelings of being compelled or obligated.*

3. ***Desiring (grasping)*** *- can range from a mild wanting to an intense urgency to get something now. The drive of ambition is an example.*

4. ***"Deserving"*** *– in the sense of "I deserve ... ," or "I don't deserve." This attachment varies in strength. It is generally easy to recognize in experiences of hurt and resentment when not gratified. Self-righteousness is another expression of this form of attachment.*

As soon as we recognize a cue, with practice, we can name it and explore what it is we are attached to, what it tells us about our ego-identities and about our needs. Practice releasing the attachment and attending to the need in a beneficial way.

HONORING EGO-ATTACHED STATES AND FEELINGS

All too often we react. We experience the distress of our ego-involvement and our emotions, expressed, or repressed. Sometimes we compound our distress by criticizing ourselves for reacting "in that way" in the first instance.

However, we do not need to be locked into reactivity. We benefit by doing something radically different. We are much better off both in the short run and the longer term to honor our attachments and our reactions.

We honor our reactions and emotions first by validating them. Our experience is our truth in the moment. This truth includes being aware of how we are thinking at that time, for instance, "I see I was criticizing myself!"

For instance, all too often instead of accepting that we reacted, we compound the problem with self-rejection, for instance, by being self-critical. We get caught up in thoughts like, "I should think before I speak. I look like a complete idiot!" Honor these thoughts, too. "Ah! Yes. I see I am being self-critical." This is a shift into meta-cognition, and it is our truth; it is what we are doing to ourselves. This recognition and acceptance are a first step towards releasing ego-attachments.

Now validate the intensity. Sometimes we react intensely, ten out of ten. Or the feelings may be vestigial, less than one out of ten, or anywhere in between. Note the intensity as in, "Phew! I'm really caught in this one." Breathe into the awareness; it may be a bodily sensation, or a more amorphous "feeling" or a thought-stream. Breathe out relaxing breaths. Allow yourself to relax.

Repeat breathing into the distress and breathing out, intentionally relaxing. Observe yourself shifting into a more relaxed state. This will require both willingness and effort, especially before you have this approach well established as a practice.

As you move into relaxation, practice self-forgiveness. Forgive yourself for reacting and being attached. It can be helpful to have a brief recitation of forgiveness, such as, "May I forgive myself for … . May I let this burden go. Let it go. Let it go." Over time you will experience a softening; this contributes to a sense of inner freedom.

Forgiveness is one aspect of honoring and is expanded in Contrast #20. Another is cultivating responsibility.

Responsibility is first the recognition and acceptance that you generated your reaction. It was not caused by external circumstances. The second aspect of responsibility is to use the experience constructively. For instance, "What can I learn that is likely to be beneficial in the future?" Another question you might address is "How do I keep (or, restore) my sense of integrity?"

We can find a certain dignity in maintaining our sense of integrity. Although our habits are such that we tend to shrink away from or ignore this challenge. This is because honoring our reactivity is opening up to our "shadow sides," aspects of ourselves we ordinarily avoid considering. Just allow that it is so and work on it.

Over time honoring our attachments and reactivity assists us to free ourselves compassionately from the burden of stress-inducing habits and beliefs.

PRACTICE EXPERIENCING NATURAL ATTACHMENT

Natural attachment seems to be quite easy to recognize experientially but difficult to describe. Assuming there is no ego-involvement, we seem to flow with the experience. Perhaps the following example does not work for you experientially. You should have a rather delicious physical-emotional experience if it does. If not, find another circumstance, where you have a comparable experience.

Imagine walking in a park. A couple approaches you with a friendly, floppy puppy, your favorite breed. Puppy rolls over and you are already delighting in feelings of fur and aliveness and softness. For me, that is a Golden Retriever puppy. There is no thought, let alone judgment involved in the immediate experience of the puppy. This is a natural attachment.

You could now practice each of the natural attachments suggested below. Recall or imagine events where you have experienced each of them without ego-attachment. Use this re-experiencing as a way to enhance your appreciation of vital human experiences. The list includes:

Affiliation* Loving	*Comfort*	*Grief*	*Rage*
Bored	*Disgust*	*Longing*	*Sad*
Caring*	*Enjoying*	*Lonely*	*Safe*
Closeness*	*Fear*	*Productive*	*Secure*

* Affiliative experiences are very wide ranging. You might wish to create your own sub-list, especially noting ways you experience natural attachment.

While I have suggested that natural attachments tend to flow, this varies situationally. Some endure and underlie the immediacy of other experiences. Affiliative experiences especially family bonding, grief at the loss of a bond, the need to "feel productive" (meaningful), feeling secure and alertness to safety (having a sense of control) all seem to occur as this experiential substrate but vary depending on the context.

SUMMARY

As a way of summarizing this Contrast, let us consider the co-occurrence of ego and natural attachments. They almost invariably co-occur. Even in our most reactive moments, we may usefully identify the natural aspect. This is worth attending to. Then we can appreciate something about ourselves that is beyond ego. Doing so can also help us identify what needs require attention.

A brief example is attachment to being on Facebook. Suppose that is your strong desire. The ego attachments may include your number of friends compared to some others and how many positive comments you get. At the same time as an aspect of caring, the wellbeing of your virtual friends can matter deeply to you as a natural attachment.

First attend to ego-attachment in the way suggested earlier. Otherwise, we are likely to stay caught up ego-involved. Our "deeper," natural feelings and attachments are then obscured. Having attended to the hook, I recognize that I do care naturally for the well-being of other people. The essential question I am addressing is, "How do I both attend to my attachments skillfully and, in the instance of the example, express caring naturally?"

Practice #17.1
Honoring Ego-Attachment

1. **Notice and name "ego"** – "hooked," "driven," "desiring," "deserving" or use any name that works for you. What matters is that you leap into awareness of the experience, instead of staying caught up in ego.

2. **Validate** –

    a. **Allowing:** Allow that whatever you are experiencing is the truth of your experience in the moment.

    b. **Intensity:** Notice the degree of intensity of the experience; name it, as in "minimal" or "powerful," or rate it, e.g. 1/10 minimal up to 10/10 powerful.

3. **Breathe** – into the feelings, emotion, thoughts, bodily sensations. Embrace the awareness, even if it is unpleasant and you want to avoid it. Allow yourself to relax at least enough to continue.

4. **Self-forgiveness** – use a recitation to release yourself from the burden of distress, no matter what form it takes. Example: "May I put this burden down," and let it go. "Let it go. Let it go. Let it go."

5. **Responsibility** – Get curious, "What can I learn from this? What could I take forward?"

Practice #17.2
Being Present to Natural Attachments

Ordinarily, ego-attachment and natural attachment co-occur. Attend to the ego aspect first, practicing releasing yourself from that attachment. Then, be present to natural attachment with appreciation. Appreciation is examined in Contrast #19. Here is a start.

Natural attachment is an amazing dimension of human experience. The more we open to these experiences, the more alive we feel – for instance, allowing joy fully, or if you are grieving, give yourself to the process of grieving.

1. Name the feeling or emotion. The list on p.123 may be helpful.

2. Take your awareness into the sensation, feeling or emotion.

3. Cherish the moment – this is your aliveness in the moment. No matter what form. This is "What Is." This you "being alive."

CONTRAST #18

EXPECTATIONS contrasted with
BEING OPEN TO OUTCOME

"WHAT IS NOT" – EXPECTATIONS

We expect things to happen. Sometimes we are conscious of our expectations. We expect it to rain when the weather forecast reads, "Rain tomorrow – 100%." However, many of our expectations are held preconsciously. We know them only when we get a pang of disappointment or a sense of resentment. She said she would call. He said he would buy my car. Neither happened. Had we not held expectations, the lack of a phone call and not selling the car would be of no account.

Expectations constitute "What Is Not" in that they reflect our definition of the future. Given that we react, we have a clear indication that we were attached to that outcome. The strength of our expectations and what is at stake for us are certainly highly variable. Wanting something to happen or to get a particular outcome is not the problem. It becomes a problem when we are attached to a particular outcome.

Suppose I have been let down by a friend. I'm feeling upset and annoyed. "Being let down" entails that I had expected him to follow through on his promise to pay back the one thousand dollars I loaned him. It is not just that I now need the money. I do, but that is the practical side of it, which we will consider further on. Rather, it is my ego-attachments that generate my distress.

To understand and work with the power of expectations, we need to be able to identify the ego-attachments that are at work. I will illustrate the point by listing a number of the ego-attachments that I had around the loan. I trusted him with the loan. "What a fool I was!" I am attached to being sensible. But then I find it difficult to say, "No." I am attached to being liked. If I refused, I would have been risking our friendship. I see that I am attached to having friends. Believing people are my friends and like me means I am worthwhile and feeling worthwhile is crucial to my sense of well-being. Without it, I am nothing.

So that example was loaded with expectations. Any time our expectations are not met, and we react, *we can actually turn our reaction into an opportunity for learning about ourselves and our ego-identities. At the same time, we learn to work with our attachments and release them. In this way we can generate an upside out of disappointment, frustration and so forth. In doing so, we continue to cultivate peace of mind and a sense of inner freedom.*

A second benefit derived from attending to our expectations is we can train ourselves to be open to outcomes. Importantly, being open to outcomes does not entail giving ourselves away. We attend to practical matters in ways that sustain our sense of integrity and do so without feeding our ego-identity. This is part of attending to "What Is."

"WHAT IS" – OPEN TO OUTCOMES

We may approach events aware we simply do not know what will happen, and we accept that the outcome is what it is, no matter what. Thus we may say we are "open to the outcome." The challenging practice is to be open to the outcome when the outcome is contrary to our expectations. Such situations may be taken as opportunities to enhance self-knowledge as well as to practice opening to the outcome.

How we approach being open to outcomes differs depending upon whether we are conscious of our expectations, or they are lurking somewhere below the surface in our subconscious. When we are conscious of our expectations, we can articulate them: I expect her to return my lawnmower tomorrow. I expect radiation treatment will cure my cancer.

Being conscious of expectations, we can prepare ourselves to be open to whatever happens, allowing that some outcomes are easier to be open to than others. If we cannot be fully open, at least we may be able to mitigate the degree of distress we experience, no matter what form it takes.

The second set of circumstances comes about when we are not aware of having expectations and we react. Feelings of disappointment or of frustration and anger, for example, reveal unmet expectations. When we think about it, we often react in these ways. She forgot to bring home the milk (I had asked her to get some!). I can't find my car key (but I always hang it on its hook!). We usually get caught up in what has gone wrong and how we feel about it. We may not even recognize that our reactions are grounded in expectations.

Instead of getting caught up in the "what is wrong," we can first catch the reaction. Second, we open to the outcome. This combined practice reduces, and over time, eliminates distress. The practices described at the end of this Contrast suggest how we can do both.

PRACTICAL CONSIDERATIONS

Being open to outcomes in no way precludes doing something about an issue. Misplaced keys and defaults on loans and so many other things still need to be addressed. Doing so skillfully entails attending to two key elements. One is to maintain our sense of integrity while not gratifying our ego. The second is to plan and execute whatever is within our control to take care of issues arising.

Having a sense of integrity is a major topic. I will only address one key point here. That is, maintaining our sense of integrity entails standing up for what matters to us, but not because we want to prove something or need other people's validation. Integrity is enacting a principle that is firmly established in our life history. For example, standing for gender equality is not a matter of justifying the principle or needing others' approval. It is sufficient that we are prepared to live by it, no matter what happens. This can be a tall order but knowing what we stand for and being prepared to abide by that is a crucial aspect of human dignity.

The second aspect, planning and executing the plan, may seem rather cold and overly rational. Being rational, that is getting beyond ego, does not seem to be popular these days. Even so, attending to what is likely to prove beneficial and avoiding what is likely to generate harm should contribute to both personal effectiveness and cultivating peace of mind (Contrast #8 discusses Planning).

It helps to recognize that we all tend to get driven by expectations. We hold expectations of ourselves as well as of other people. Likewise, other people hold expectations of us as well as of themselves. Distress around unmet expectations can arise from any of these directions. Responding to them as expectations rather than taking them personally can alleviate a lot of distress.

Be prepared for other people to be upset with us for not reacting. Far from garnering support, all too often staying cool is taken as a sign we don't care, or we are "above it." It is important to both validate the other person's feelings and to maintain our integrity by asserting what matters to us. This could play out in a number of ways - imagine a friend being upset at us for staying cool:

"What's wrong with you! Don't you care or something?"

In such a situation, validate their feelings and assert what matters to you: "I get it you're upset with me for not being angry. Does it seem like I don't care? It does matter to me, but I just don't want to get caught up in anger."

SUMMARY

Bear in mind that this Contrast is about reducing distress by not getting hooked on expectations. Rather we want to cultivate the ability to handle expectations with ease by releasing attachments, being open to outcomes and dealing with practicalities.

Practice #18.1
Attending to Consciously-held Expectations

1. On becoming aware of an expectation, inspect it. This is bringing it into meta-cognitive awareness (p.17). Example, meta-cognitively, you note to yourself, "Ah! I am holding such-and-such expectation."

2. Release its power, "It may not turn out that way. Yes, other outcomes are possible."

3. Attend to attachments:

    a. Identify the attachments: "What is it going to mean to me if it turns out differently?" "How strongly am I attached?"

    b. Validate the attachments: they are as they are; that is so.

    c. Release the attachments: soften to them. Hold them with compassion. Just recognizing them is a big step towards softening.

4. Open to outcome: Create the intention in your mind to be open to the outcome, for example, "I hope ... (desired outcome). I recognize other outcomes are possible. May I be open to whatever arises."

Practice #18.2
Surprised by Expectations, Opening to the Outcome

1. Notice "Reacting." Resentment, frustration, impatience, and disappointment are particularly useful indicators of unmet expectations.

2. Breathe and validate the reaction. Breathe into the tightness in your body that comes with the reaction. Validate your reaction by taking your awareness into your feelings. "Yes, I am feeling... ." That is your truth in the moment.

3. Identify the expectation, "I was expecting ... ."

4. Attend to attachments:

    a. Identify the attachments: "What does it mean to me that it turned out 'this' way?" "How strong are those attachments?"

    b. Validate the attachments: they are as they are; that is so.

    c. Release the attachments: soften to them. Hold them with compassion. Just recognizing them is a big step to softening. In softening, you are opening to having encountered the unexpected.

All the while practice relaxing breathing: take a deep breath in and relax with a longer breath out. Let your muscles relax throughout your body

CONTRAST #19

HAPPINESS contrasted with *APPRECIATING*

"WHAT IS NOT" – THE STATE OF HAPPINESS

You might feel surprised to see the happiness on the "What Is Not" side of the scales of awareness. If we seek to live in a state of happiness – that is, being happy as much as possible, we only notice happiness in contrast to being in some form of unhappiness. In the moment, however, we may not recognize that we are making a comparison in the first place.

All too often, we use our state of being as a measuring stick, say to assess our quality of life. Note that doing this subjects us to a continuing process of definition, in this case comparing one state with another. We then live according to the "What Is Not," our definition.

We create dissatisfaction by measuring our lives with happiness as a dimension, represented as: happy <===> unhappy. Making comparisons alone distorts our immediate experience and comparing frequently generates distress.

Two sources account for the distress. One is our propensity to notice and get hooked into the negative. Bear in mind this propensity has major survival value in and of itself. Yet it can generate a lot of dissatisfaction when it is applied to otherwise non-threatening circumstances - no tigers lurking except in our minds.

The second reason is that we tend to become ego-identified with particular states of being. This can generate all kinds of havoc. A couple of examples. If I believe I deserve to be happy, I am prone to resentment when my expectations are not met. If I believe happiness is tied to financial success or depends on possessions, I am unlikely to ever feel truly satisfied, and hence am never finally happy. There are so many possible ways for our attachments, manifestations of our ego-identity, to generate dissatisfaction and unhappiness. Find examples that work for you. Identity comparisons you make that set you up to experience distress, such as comparing yourself with someone else and coming up short.

*There is Wisdom in not seeking happiness; rather allow happiness to arise as a by-product of your practice. Instead, cultivate appreciation. "Valuing" is synonymous with appreciation when experienced emotionally or as a feeling, and **not defined** in terms of money or possession.*

"WHAT IS" – APPRECIATING

"Appreciation," as I am intending the word to be taken, is only as "immediate experience." It is a way of experiencing connection with whatever we are appreciating. This is not concerned with past or future. There is no story, although we may subsequently build a story around the experience.

Appreciation is a practice of Discriminating Wisdom. The Discrimination is in taking ourselves out of the realm of "What Is Not," which is established particularly by defining and comparing. It takes us into the realm of valuing our immediate experience. The Wisdom is that we are cultivating our capacity to feel fully alive in the moment, to be at ease and sense our connection with "What Is," the immediacy of the moment. We may experience the sacred, the divine, or a sense of beauty in the most ordinary of moments through this practice. We are alive and aware at such times.

As mentioned, appreciation is only experiential. Any words we might use to describe the experience also define it. This matters in two ways. One, I want to highlight the interplay between language and experience. Language can only guide you to the entrance into the ballpark; you enter the ballpark on your own. You can appreciate imagined experiences, memories, and present time experiences.

Other words I associate with appreciation besides valuing are "cherishing" and "embracing." Embedded in this experience is the sense of connection. Take some time now to recollect events or circumstance that you have appreciated in the past. Through your imagination or using a photograph, for instance, endeavor to recreate a sense of appreciation.

The second way this matters is in sharing these experiences with other people. Certainly, we can be "in appreciation" in moments of shared silence. On the other hand, we may well want to talk about the experience. Strive to express appreciation descriptively or metaphorically. The use of adjectives, beliefs, and opinions, such as, "What a wonder of nature," or "How magnificent!" while expressive, take away from sharing appreciation.

The experience of appreciation does not usually endure for ordinary events. On the other hand, where we have established an emotional bond, we may well spend considerable periods of time in appreciation. In longer-term experiences, appreciation can easily get combined with ego-investment, perhaps with sexuality added to the mix, for instance, in feeling attracted to another person.

We have the choice between striving for happiness or any comparable state and cultivating the immediate experience of appreciating our lives as we unfold them moment-by-moment. Certainly much depends on the effort we put into focusing on the experience of appreciation. Much of the struggle goes out of life as we lay down a path in this way. The experience of happiness, not the state of happiness, may arise as we imbue each moment with appreciation. We may have other forms of emotional experience nuanced by the ways in which we encounter the world.

Having a Contrast devoted to the practice of appreciation is intentional. Appreciating serves our well-being. We are fostering the shift from being caught up in "What Is Not" to becoming increasingly engaged with the "What Is" of our immediate experience. The practice here extends Practice #9 by encouraging appreciation of things we have made ordinary. Young children often find delight in things we no longer notice, such as the buzzing of a bee or soap bubbles in the washing-up water. The following practice makes use of the magic of "If," introduced in Contrast #13, p.98. This approach helps us to re-awaken a childhood sense of discovery.

Practice #19
Deepening Appreciation

Practice many times a day (minimally three):

Focus on ordinary things and ordinary events - people just walking around, the traffic, trees. Once you are appreciating the moment, focus on that experience, breathe it in, take it in as deeply as you can.

When you are aware of "ordinariness" without a sense of appreciation, apply the magic of "If" by asking yourself the question, "If I could appreciate anything about ... , what would I appreciate?" Observe your mind, see what bubbles up. Appreciate whatever shows up, focus on the experience, breathe it in, taking it in as deeply as you can.

If nothing bubbles up, focus on being alive to the experience and the sense(s) you are using and delight in them. Focus on that experience, breathe it in, take it in as deeply as you can.

And one more level, apply the magic of "If" to situations in which you find nothing to appreciate in the situation (For the magic of "if," see p.98). It can be quite amazing how with practice we can find something to appreciate under even increasingly trying circumstances.

CONTRAST #20

BEING JUSTIFIED
contrasted with *PRACTICING FORGIVENESS*

"WHAT IS NOT" – JUSTIFYING

Examining how we justify ourselves may well be a topic we strenuously want to avoid. However, if we are willing to observe ourselves, we notice just how much of our thinking is devoted to justifying our perspective.

Justifying defines us as being right. We will be right in our opinions about other people, about our own actions and characteristics or anything else you care to mention. Even when we find that we have been wrong about something, we will tend to justify why we have been wrong.

There is a neurological aspect to this. Our thinking is structured so that we cannot be wrong in our own minds. Our brains operate like lifeboats; they are self-righting. It seems like we can only be logical. We are wired this way. When we say something like, "He is not being rational," or "She is illogical," or "I was so stupid," we obscure that we are simply being right in our own minds, no matter that our thinking generates distress. Our thinking follows its own internal logic, no matter how illogical it seems either in hindsight or from another frame of reference.

When we are locked up in a frame of reference, we are stuck. Thus, when we are feeling justified, we are justified. No question, except perhaps from our critics. Our prefrontal cortex is fully engaged in justifying how we think, our emotional reactions and our behavior, all of which are manifestations of our belief system. It is our belief system that usually drives our default way of making sense of whatever is going on. Observing ourselves, we can learn to identify our patterns of justification. These patterns are strongly associated with our core beliefs, and they support our ego.

You may recognize here the analogy of the Elephant and the Rider from the chapter on the brain. In justifying, the Elephant leads the way. The Rider uses justification to explain why the Elephant is cavorting around or doing whatever it is doing.

LEVELS OF JUSTIFICATION

Justification may be thought of as patterns operating at three broad levels. Thinking in terms of these levels can help us recognize what we are doing. Then we may choose to shift into a process that usefully starts with forgiveness.

1) **Reacting** – The first level is comprised of our immediate reactions, as illustrated above in terms of our brains being self-righting, like lifeboats. "I didn't mean that!" "Oh, you just don't understand," "Don't make me mad," are common justifications for our reactions.

2) **Lifestyle** – The second, broader level of justification endures longer — hours to years — and encompasses how we live. No matter whether we think of ourselves as being happy or unhappy, these patterns justify our lifestyles, our relationships, our work, and our recreational activities. To the extent we feel happy and satisfied, we justify that with an explanation. If we are unhappy or face challenges in our lives, we will justify that, too.

3) **Life history** – The third level goes the deepest. It is the frame that shapes significant aspects of our lives. A simple illustration of this level is that of being the adult son of an alcoholic father. "I" can elaborate that fact to justify everything that is difficult in "my" life. Notice that such ideas are expressions of belief, and whatever our beliefs may be, we generally live from within them. They appear to us as Truth and Reality. To the extent we feel distressed, we are trapped within them.

We are only able to recognize what we are doing when we shift our frame of reference. *We can make this shift by applying meta-cognitive awareness. That is, we recognize at the immediate level, "Oh! 'That' is what I am doing." Perhaps I recognize that I am feeling jealous or threatened, for example. We can apply this awareness to any level of justification. This is the moment in which we can practice Discriminating Wisdom and lay a path with forgiveness.*

"WHAT IS" – PRACTICING FORGIVENESS

First, I will describe what I intend in recommending the practice of forgiveness and then explain why it is warranted as an ongoing practice. This goes considerably beyond remedying harm, although remedying harm may be a significant part of the process.

FORGIVENESS

Forgiveness — **PUTTING DOWN THE BURDEN OF DISTRESS.**

In forgiving, we are manifesting Discriminating Wisdom. Forgiveness does not say what was done is okay, no matter by whom. It did matter. Forgiven or unforgiven, it still matters, but it can matter in two distinct ways. One way of mattering is that distress is perpetuated as anger, guilt, resentment, denial, shame, self-justification, and self-righteousness. We are compounding harm by distressing about it. We need to forgive ourselves for that, too.

The second way forgiveness is approached is in three "directions": first, forgiving ourselves for inflicting harm. Second, we seek forgiveness from those who we have harmed, and, finally, forgive those who have harmed us. For ourselves, we seek to release ourselves from the burdens of guilt and shame for our actions. For those we have harmed, we take responsibility and ask directly for forgiveness. We can also consider how they might want harms remedied. Finally, for those who have harmed us, we may confront them, and we might ask for a remedy. But allow it is sufficient to ask. They may or may not accede to any request. Or, for both harming others and being harmed, we may forgive these harms internally and in this way put the burden of the past down.

A BROADER SENSE OF FORGIVENESS

I am focusing here on how we generate distress for ourselves. We will consider all three levels of distress, reactivity, life-style and our life histories and bring the practice of forgiveness to each one.

*1. **Forgiving Reactivity** – In Contrast #17 on p.121, I referred to "hooked," "driven," "desiring" (grasping) and "deserving" as broad categories of attachment. We need to start by forgiving ourselves for the reactivity of attachment. This gives us the freedom to open to moment-by-moment experiences. Releasing the need to justify at this level affects all the "bigger" items that need to be resolved.*

Just owning up to reacting as in, "Oh! I reacted. I am so sorry," is one way of attending to the interpersonal side. What response is warranted is highly contextual. At the same time, we also need to attend to whatever is internal. Suppose I feel guilty for reacting. I want to forgive myself for reacting. Having done so, I can then more easily attend to whatever else may need to be remedied.

There is also the matter of other people's behavior towards you. Yogi Bhajan offered advice that is integral to forgiveness:

> *If you are willing to look at another person's behavior towards you as a reflection of the state of their relationship with themselves rather than a statement about your value as a person, then you will, over a period of time, cease to react at all.*

You are no longer carrying that burden when you do not take the other person personally. By all means hold them responsible for their actions as needs may be. Even as you hold them responsible, you can also hold them in the heart of compassion.

2. Forgiving Lifestyle – *Perhaps lifestyle carries the connotations of how we want our lives to be. There may be a discrepancy with how we are actually living. It can be quite useful to recognize what comparisons we are making, and we need to forgive ourselves. For example, perhaps we really do not like our job or our boss. We may know what we would like. Then we compare our current situation with an imagined alternative and increase our level of dissatisfaction. We benefit by forgiving ourselves for pulling ourselves down and generating our own distress. At the same time, we can look for another job if we choose to. It's just that we do not distress ourselves over the one we currently have.*

Anger, blame, criticalness, dissatisfaction, envy, guilt, jealousy, liking, disliking, resentment, shame, and superiority (self-righteousness) are prominent among the more enduring experiences that can be associated with our lifestyle. Practice Discriminating Wisdom by shifting from "something wrong" to entering a process of forgiveness:

1. *Acceptance, "I have taken on this burden."*

2. *Intention, "I intend to lay it down."*

3. *Beneficial need, "What do I need to attend to so I can move on?"*

The needs show up in three ways: the need for self-forgiveness, the need to forgive others and the need for forgiveness by others. For some people "others" could be needing God's forgiveness. What needs to be forgiven can take many forms. Likewise, there are many ways to forgive. There are two attitudes that militate against forgiveness — guilt and shame.

Guilt and Shame: Feeling guilty, ashamed, or beating ourselves up does not make us a better person. That is so no matter how much we want to believe that self-flagellation is beneficial. It is more likely to serve as fuel for the fire of self-righteousness.

An alternative is to take responsibility for ourselves, our actions, our feelings, and our attitudes. Taking responsibility can be approached through:

1. ***Acknowledging**, as in, "Yes, I have done 'this'." Instead of "done," we may need to insert "I hold 'this' attitude, or "I have 'these' feelings, or "I have 'these' thoughts."*

2. ***Seeking to remedy**, as in, "How might I remedy...?" Make a plan.*

3. ***Taking action,** carry out the plan. If you want another to make amends to you, or if you are seeking forgiveness from them, you can ask. How they respond is beyond your control. Allow that it is sufficient you have asked, given that you enter the process whole-heartedly and maintain your sense of integrity. If seeking or offering amends directly would put you at physical risk, then you might consider having a third party, such as a trusted friend, be your witness.*

When another person is the perpetrator, use the principle articulated by Yogi Bhajan above as your guide. Sustain your sense of integrity and show respect for the perpetrator – this is not respect in terms of what they have done, but it is a respect for their being a living person. They have their own suffering and their own distress. We have at best a limited understanding of what history their lives represent. We no longer need to judge them to justify our feelings. We can put that burden down.

*3. **Life History** – Many people carry burdens from their past, and they continue to live in reaction to that past. As a personal example, I survived my mother by striving to please her. That was seventy-plus years ago. Even so, for me not to do what another person wants still carries a sense of doing something wrong. Thus, I continue to practice forgiveness of myself for this drive to please and take the risk of asserting what matters to me.*

However, there is a downside to leaving the Prison of Justification. All too often we have learned to use our past to justify the present. Such justification enables us to avoid taking responsibility for ourselves, including not taking risks. It also allows us to indulge ourselves and avoid taking other people truly into account. The self-servingness of an unresolved past and the justificatory beliefs that sustain it tend to hold us in a powerful grip.

You might think of justification metaphorically as tramping down a broad, downhill path. Certainly, justifying allows us to stumble around an old, familiar path. Forgiveness has us laying a path uphill, uphill in the sense that the practice of forgiveness requires sustained effort combining compassion with letting go of the past.

We are left with a hard choice. We can continue with whatever coping strategies we have developed. Or we take the challenge to lay down a new path: forgive the past, forgive ourselves, forgive others, seek forgiveness, and take care of ourselves. Sustain integrity and embrace freedom.

Practice #20.1
Countering Self-Justification and Beating Ourselves Up

This practice is intended to counter defaulting to self-justification and mental and emotional self-flagellation. Either can occur as Default Modes of Thought (see list on p.37 in Contrast #4).

Recite the follow prayer (or your own equivalent). Doing so shifts you into meta-cognitive awareness. Allow yourself to settle and feel centered. Then enter the practice of forgiveness (#20.2)

Bury the Dead
Forgive the Past
Open to the Present
Cultivate the Future

Practice #20.2
Forgiving

1. **Acknowledge** – "I am conscious I am carrying ... (name the burden)."

2. **Compassion** – Bring compassion to the burden; allow yourself to care about the pain and distress experienced, no matter whose.

3. **Forgiving** – Breathe deeply into your chest. Relax on the out breath, at the same time reciting: "May I forgive... . May I be free of this burden; May I let it go." Repeat this blessing a number of times.

4. **Amends** – Make amends where you can but skillfully so that you cultivate benefit.

5. **Difficulty and Resistance** – When you encounter difficulty or resistance to forgiving something in particular, practice forgiving yourself for having the difficulty in the first place (Review Contrast #3 re. Resistance, as needed).

IN CONCLUSION

WHAT THEN SHALL WE PRACTICE?

The practice of *Discriminating Wisdom* allows us to cultivate peace of mind and a sense of inner freedom. To the extent we feel emotional distress, our habitual modes of thought keep us trapped. That we experience this type of distress informs us that we are imprisoned within walls of "What Is Not," constructed by our own defining. The alternative offered here applies *Discriminating Wisdom* to the "What Is" of our immediate experience and guides how we lay our path from there.

If we address the question, "What then shall we practice?" there are a small number of skills that are essential for each of us to develop in laying our own path. This chapter highlights key skills. Please consider how you will work with them. As you do, you will realize for yourself when and where you need to direct your attention and effort.

Hiking up a mountain provides a metaphor for the journey. I presented the forest metaphor early in the introductory chapter. Now I want to emphasize laying a new path, one that heads up a mountain. "Up a mountain" because when you choose to shift from following the old path of "What Is Not" to laying the new path of living "What Is," you are climbing the steep and demanding Mountain of Self.

No matter whether you like hiking or not, in terms of life's journey you have been hiking around an all-too-familiar trail in the forest at the bottom of the mountain. As you climb above the tree line, you will encounter the spaciousness of the upper slope. Increasingly free, you also find peace of mind.

View the mountain as the totality of our ego-attachments. Before making the shift, how we live is defined by our attachments, beliefs, and habits. If we choose to make the shift, we intentionally reframe the mountain as something to explore. We transform the mountain, with all its rocky outcrops, boulders, beliefs, and idiosyncrasies, into opportunities supporting us in our climb.

Although exactly how we lay our path is up to us individually, there are a few basic skills needed by all climbers. Learning these skills is anything but a quick fix; they are a life-long practice. The wolf-pack of ego, mental habits, desires, aversions, and the appeal of delusion are always somewhere around. The consolation is that the further up the slope you get, the more the howls of the wolves recede into the distance. Let us review the basic skills required for climbing the Mountain of Self.

BASIC SKILLS FOR CLIMBING THE MOUNTAIN OF SELF

SHIFTING FROM DISTRESS TO OPPORTUNITY

The Mountain of Self is a solid mass of beliefs and meanings, ego-identity, and ego-attachments. This is "What Is Not." As hiker, we distress ourselves one way or another with beliefs that we took on early in life, and we have deluded ourselves ever since. In effect, we have lived in the belief that we are both the mountain and the hiker. Now we intend to be the hiker only.

As hiker, we have the opportunity to shift to being present to "What Is." "What Is" is our immediate experience of encountering the mountain, but no longer in the defined form, the mountain of "who we are." Rather we generate for ourselves an ongoing series of opportunities to explore.

Both being willing to make this shift and practicing doing so on a day-by-day, moment-by-moment basis is key. It takes both effort and persistence to get this shift going. Given daily practice, allow yourself up to a full year to notice the shift coming easily.

INITIATING THE SHIFT

Recognition – *Recognizing what is going within in you is the crucial moment. This is the beginning of the shift. Without this, nothing happens. This is the shift, metaphorically, from being caught up in a day-dream, stumbling on a root, and cursing either the root for being there or yourself for being careless. You shift to awareness of what you are doing mentally and your intention to be present.*

Duration – *Duration is critical to making the shift. The reactive system can take as little as 40/1,000's of a second to kick into action. The response system takes as much as half a second to activate. Furthermore, you experience whatever emotional charge is associated with your* reaction. You need time, 5 seconds, 10 seconds, maybe longer, to shift into meta-cognition and choose how to respond.

Take on the adage such as, "Count to ten." As you count, breathe relaxing breaths. We often tell children to do this, but seldom do so ourselves. Yet there is great wisdom in this practice. You are allowing your hormonal system, that prepares the body for fight-or-flight, to settle down. You have created both the time and space you need for the prefrontal cortex do its work. At a conscious level, you are considering your options.

Being in Truth – Allowing that whatever is true for you experientially in the moment is true is another crucial component of the shift. This shifts you away from defining your reaction. For example, "I can't climb this mountain. It is too difficult!" Instead, you recognize and acknowledged the truth of the "What Is" of your immediate experience, as in, "Ah! I see I am telling myself 'I can't climb this mountain'." Now, continue the shift by making this an opportunity to explore what is going on for you.

Opportunities – We can take our reactivity, our likes and dislikes, our feelings, especially unpleasant ones, and our judgments as opportunities to see what path we have been following and to choose the path we want to lay now.

Opportunities exist in adopting an attitude of curiosity. This attitude brings ordinary events to life. For instance, when you feel upset with something, you might ask with a genuine sense of wanting to find out, "Wow! How did I bring 'upset' into being?" Such a question can shift the whole experience. You might explore further with questions such as, "What am I doing to myself with those thoughts?" Or, if what is going on seems rather obscure, ask, "What is going on here?" "What is this experience?" Experiment – see what works for you in seeking to cultivate benefit.

Certainly, a key part of the process is to frame moment-by-moment experiences as opportunities. Even with this optimism, each of us will encounter three cliffs on the way up the mountain.

THREE CLIFFS

As we shift from dwelling in the forest of "What Is Not" to exploring the upward slopes of "What Is," we encounter three cliffs: resistance, the negativity bias and default modes of thought. Scaling these does not make laying the path any easier; rather it makes it possible. Each of these "cliffs" is covered in detail elsewhere in the book. I highlight them to emphasize the need to be prepared for when you encounter them. They stand between you and peace of mind and inner freedom.

The Cliff of Resistance – Your brain conspiring with your ego will stand in the way of you making the shift (see Contrast #3). It may even be difficult to get handholds on this one. That is because habitual modes of thought and reaction operate preconsciously. But as soon as you notice yourself resisting, make that an opportunity to be in truth with resisting. Suppose you have the thought, "I can't be bothered with shifting right now," then this is exactly where you need to make the effort right in the moment.

Do not simply believe the voice that tells you that you cannot be bothered. You are being fed a line by some old, self-indulgent voice. Make a handhold on this cliff by using your meta-cognitive ability, "Ah-ha! I hear 'that voice' (name it if you care to) telling me, 'I can't be bothered.' So, what is going on here?" Now you are exploring the immediate experience of resistance. Find out what you need to do to let it go and move on.

The Cliff of Negativity – We have considered our negativity bias at a number of points (c.f.: p. 2 Evolution, and p.38). Negativity manifests in so many different forms but all of them define how we encounter events as they arise – that is, with a negative spin even if the motive is to make something better.

Unless it is a real emergency, go into the experience, not the definition, "What am I experiencing right now?" "What is true for me in this moment?" "What am I trying to do?" What can you now do to cultivate benefit?

The Cliff of Default Thinking – It can be very instructive to observe what our thinking does when we are not focused on a task. We can make use of this awareness to learn about ourselves, identify underlying needs and find skillful means to attend to those needs.

The Chapter on The Brain considered this topic in terms of the Elephant and the Rider. Contrast #12 suggested a number of ways for examining how we tell our stories, such as identifying the roles we play and the qualities we show (See p. 92). Applying this same mode of analysis to our default thinking can open up a deep understanding of both what we are doing to ourselves and how we are doing it.

AS A FINAL ENCOURAGEMENT

An implication of all the suggestions offered in this book is that we are in training to be highly tuned into ourselves. Lest you think this is promoting self-absorption or self-preoccupation, that is not so. It is when we are defending ourselves or promoting our ideas or berating ourselves that we are self-absorbed.

As we get skilled in the practice of Discriminating Wisdom, we find ourselves to be increasingly at ease, to be able to attend to "stuff" as it comes up. We are able to meet the vicissitudes of life with a certain lightness and with compassion, love, and abiding appreciation.

As a final encouragement, you can come to dwell in the open uplands. With practice, you live increasingly in the freedom of immediate experience. We foster the quality of our experience by practicing appreciation (see: Contrast #19). Here I only want to reiterate the value of the practice as a key aspect of cultivating Discriminating Wisdom. I recommend you make it a salient aspect of the path you lay. In practicing appreciation, you foster joy, love, compassion, and the experience of connection.

We have the capacity to both cultivate well-being for one another and make choices in regard to ourselves. And for those choices, as Mary Oliver put it in a poem addressing a grasshopper,[3] "What do you plan to do with this one wild and precious life?"

"And what do you plan to do with your one wild and precious life"?

---

3   "The Summer Day," Mary Oliver, *House of Light*, Beacon Press, 1990.